Living as a Dead Man

Life Lessons Gained from Losing One Life to Receiving a Greater Purpose

Jeff Lester

CONTENTS

ABOUT THE COVER

The cover of Living as a Dead Man is a painting by Laura Bartlett Jurica. She painted it while in Greece.

Her work spoke to me when she posted it on Facebook in 2008. Laura graciously gave me the painting after I commented on how it moved me regarding my journey with ALS. It has hung in my bedroom as a reminder ever since. Here's what I wrote:

> When I saw your painting, it depicted how when ALS enters your life you become much like the man in the small boat who has some control with the rudder, but for the most part, he's at the mercy of the river's current. It's more than that. I imagine this man is somehow chained in the boat so while he occasionally has visitors including people helping him by giving him sustenance and cleaning his vessel, he's alone. For the most part, he is alone watching life float by, sometimes at a distance and other times as he gets close to the riverbank. Sometimes he even ties up to a dock but scarcely participates in the festivities since he can't leave the boat. He can only watch others enjoying their lives. He wishes he had lived life differently before he was chained to the boat. He knows his leaky, old craft eventually will succumb to the river drowning him as he watches people on the shore. This is what having ALS is like.

Laura Bartlett Jurica is a Sikeston, Missouri born artist that now lives in Florida. Laura is an award-winning photographer and published travel writer who has taken her love of travel and art to create culture inspired pieces that embrace the world we all depend on. She aims to combine her love of Art, culture, and her diverse heritage into works of art that remind her viewers, underneath the clothes and traditions of our cultures we are all the same.

www.facebook.com/juricacreativeartdesign

ACKNOWLEDGEMENTS

Angi Payne Sutton served as my editor and mentor for my first book project. Her invaluable contribution and guidance throughout this process gave me the ability to create a professional finished product. More important was her encouragement for me to tell my story. Who knew when God brought us together as classmates and friends in Sikeston Middle School four decades ago that He had such great collaboration planned for us. I am blessed to have Angi as my editor and friend.

Team Gleason replaced my 20-year-old HeadMouse in 2018. Without their grant paying for its replacement, finishing this book would have been impossible!

http://www.teamgleason.org/

Kelsey Lester served as my initial editor and reader. She let me know where my story was going right and where it might need more work. Her input was vital.

Jordan Lester and Emily Lester photographed the artwork used for the cover and assisted in its design, which was essential in creating it and producing a professional cover for the book.

Thank you to Chesterfield Minuteman Press for copying and spiral binding the beta copies of my book!

https://www.chesterfield.minutemanpress.com/

A special thanks go out to my beta readers who helped refine my work. They are Laura Bailey, Dr. Sara Chaney, Greg Lester, Clay Bailey, Dr. Karen Hopkins, Lisa Lester, Dr. Jack Hopkins, and Emily Lester.

I am deeply grateful for all the teachers, coaches, family, and friend's parents who helped guide and encourage me to strive to be the best I could be. Each of you played a unique role in shaping my character and story.

To all the people who have supported and lifted me up in prayer throughout my journey with ALS, you forever have my gratitude. Without your love over all these years, I would not have succeeded in overcoming ALS and living to tell of my triumphant victory.

I want to give a special thanks to my friend, Jon Blair, who helped me reconnect with the significant men that influenced my life even though they are gone from this world. He also brought me closer to God in a singular way by sharing communion with me in my home. Where two gathers in Jesus' name, He will also be there. Jon also directly inspired me to write the chapter on endurance. I feel blessed he was able to read my first draft through that chapter before his passing. You are missed my friend until we meet again!

Finally, to all my brothers and sisters in ALS, thank you for inspiring me with your courage and strength. We have battled this monster called ALS, Lou Gehrig's Disease, or MND together in a valiant fight against impossible odds. Many have fallen over my over twenty-five years with this dreadful disease. I hope my book brings honor to you and inspires our newest family members to take up the mantle to finally rid this world of this horrible disease. I pray that my story is one of the last ALS tales.

BOOK PATRONS

Jay Greenwood - Friend, Teammate & O-line brother

Jimmy and Jera Lincoln

Jerry Aufdenberg
In Memory of Scott Aufdenberg ALS

Darlene Eck
In Memory of Peggy Sue Cline Farni ALS

Leslie Corley

Denise Murphy
In Memory of Doyle Murphy, ALS 1982
In Honor of Robert Murphy ALS Child Caregiver

Mark Howser, Glacier Park Trading Co

Carol Munson
In Memory of Mike Munson 1953-2017 ALS for 5yrs-4months

Michelle Etheredge
In Memory of my dad, Sydney Palladino

Barb Satterthwaite

Daniel Rathe
In Loving Memory of the Stanley/Harrell Families fallen to FALS

Pamela Parana
In Memory of Lawrence E. Carlson

Marge Blair
In Memory of Jon Blair

Judy Brock Bilyeu

Cay Sikes

Bonnie Stewart

Sharon Ferrell

Mark and Julie Snowbarger
In Memory of Johnny Pittman and his 3-year battle with ALS

Deneke' Borders Murphy
In Honor of the Sikeston High School Class of 1988
In Memory of our classmates who have gone before us.

Jo Stockly
In Memory of my hero, Gary Stockly

Rhonda Brodbeck
In Memory of my husband, Mark Mendelsohn

Garrett J Smith

Kristen Norlund
In Memory of my dad, Larry Norlund

Janey Sailors Radford

Tim Hughes

Kathy French

Karen Aufdenberg Reynolds
In Memory of her parents, Gene and Alice Aufdenberg

Michele Bailey

Joann and Murray Sullivan

The Roegman Family
In Memory of Cousin Harvey

To Mom and Dad
For teaching me love and making me a man

To Lisa, my wife, my Wonder Woman
For proving what true love means

To my daughters
For proving what pure love is
You are my heart, my greatest feat, my legacy

INTRODUCTION

The day they diagnosed me with ALS started my darkest days. Life was over in my mind. Still single and just before my twenty-seventh birthday, the prospects were bleak. Within a month, I broke a leg, transferred my job to St. Louis, and moved twice. The ALS specialist squashed any glimmer of hope in December 1993. The doctor informed me I would be lucky to see the age of thirty, so plan a big party as a pseudo funeral. Who would blame me for giving up? Something happened on the way to my early funeral.

God had other plans.

My story is about the destruction of the life I expected to live and rebuilding a new, more purposeful life out of its ashes. Along the way, I weather massive storms and overcome what seem insurmountable odds. It occurs while I endure the daily challenges created by the devastation from one of the worst diseases someone can experience.

Ultimately, it is a story about being led into the light emerging from the darkness that clouded my life even before ALS entered it. It was hard and trying. I learned to focus on the blessings in this life instead of what I lost and the difficulties I face. I share the lessons learned and what is essential to living a happy and fulfilling life with a higher purpose. Anyone who struggles with a problem in their life will hopefully find inspiration from my story to overcome and see better days.

The real journey is my separation from and rediscovering God in my life. It's about gaining strength to endure negativity, pain, and whatever else life throws at you to bring you down and defeat you.

Living as a Dead Man is my journey with ALS, also known as Lou Gehrig's Disease and MND around the world. Doctors diagnosed me with ALS over twenty-five years ago. However, this book is not about ALS. While you read about certain aspects of my disease, it's only a supporting role. You could substitute any other condition someone struggles with in their life.

Within the story, I attempt to pass along the lessons learned and how my struggles reshaped my life. I didn't write this book intending for it to be a Christian nonfiction book. It wasn't until I relived the earlier years and the story unfolded as I wrote that I realized ALS brought me closer to God. More significant, I discovered the meaning of life and that we all have a higher purpose.

Staring out the window
Imagining to be free
Set adrift in the beautiful world
God sets before me

The sun so bright
Shining through my tree
Painting my eyes with loveliness
Where else would I want to be

Ablaze with color
I yearn to frolic in the leaves
Pondering to myself
Why doesn't everyone else believe

The majesty of the world is lost
On many people today
Why can't they awaken
And hear what I have to say

Our time on earth
What a short-lived story
Don't waste one moment of it
Before going to His glory

Staring out the window
Imagining to be free
Sunset on this glorious day
Maybe tomorrow it becomes reality

SECTION 1

LEARNING TO LIVE AGAIN

You have taken off your old self ... and have put on the new self, which is being renewed in knowledge in the image of its Creator.

Colossians 3:9-10 (NIV)

Who would blame me for giving up?

God had other plans.

PROLOGUE

LOST IN THE WILDERNESS

Darkness cannot drive out darkness: only light can do that.
Hate cannot drive out hate: only love can do that.

Martin Luther King Jr. from A Testament of Hope:
The Essential Writings and Speeches

My struggle and separation from God began over seven years before my diagnosis with ALS. It is critical to my life's journey and my experience with ALS.

Walking out of my World History exam, I feel self-confident about how I did. My attention already turns toward blowing off steam with my brothers at Phi Kappa Psi. That's until I see HIM waiting outside the classroom. He's a university administrator and renowned biochemistry professor at Ole Miss, better known as Uncle Maurice, my dad's sister's husband. My pace slows. I stare at my shuffling feet, trying to extend my last few seconds of youth. I fear the pain I'm sure the Grim Reaper brings. Time seems to both hasten and slow.

"Jeff!" he shouts over the clamoring mass of students spilling out into the hallway. It shatters my existence, dragging me into a new reality. "Your dad's in the hospital. You may not make it before he dies. Your aunt is getting ready to drive you up because we don't want you getting in an accident going home." During the moment's fog, I don't respond. I dash toward my dorm, Deaton Hall, weaving through the mob of students in my way. Uncle Maurice tries to keep up as I hurry back to grab stuff and get on the road north to Sikeston, Missouri. He wants to hand me off to Aunt Susan. They don't want me to leave on my own when I am ready. The only thing that jars me out of my haze is his reminder to pack clothes for Dad's funeral.

Dad's death is not surprising to our family, but it shocks my world. He contracted a mysterious lung disease, later diagnosed as pulmonary fibrosis, while serving as a dentist in the Navy during the Vietnam War. In 1968, he had a rare, fatal illness around the age of twenty-seven. Dad suddenly lost fifty percent of his lung capacity for no apparent reason, and they told him he didn't have long to live.

Dad lived his life on his terms, not according to the dire prediction. He achieved this so successfully; it wasn't until the early 1980s I became aware a serious issue existed. Even then, everything continued as usual.

Despite being advised to stay in six months longer for him to receive medical retirement benefits, Dad left the Navy on the regular schedule since his business was set up in Missouri. He established a successful dental practice in Sikeston while being active in social and physical activities from golf to hunting. Dad was an involved father, including coaching his children in sports. Even with him having a debilitating lung disease for most of my life, confronting Dad's death when he's forty-five is shocking from my perspective.

In October, a few months after I left for college, I met Mom and Dad in Memphis. They revealed the gravity of his failing condition. We met in the parking garage where his appointment was that day.

First seeing Mom's tear-swollen eyes foretold the bad news. When she opened the van door exposing Dad, pale and struggling to breathe on oxygen, my curtain of innocence came down.

Our talk took place in a parking garage because his exhaustion made it impossible to go anywhere else. Dad told me he was dying. He made me promise to continue to do well in school and live as if nothing was happening back home. It was a difficult request to honor because my heart desperately wanted to go home to spend every moment with him. Out of reverence for his wishes, I did what he asked.

It's easy pretending everything is normal while living a typical college life. However, I didn't confront losing the most impactful man in my life who shaped the man I became.

On the occasions I traveled home, reality slapped me hard in the face. I lived in an alternate reality because my heart would have forced me home. Each time I went back, I entered the painful dimension of Dad's physical deterioration and his march toward death. During these visits, I became his physical protector. He wouldn't go out in public without me because I had the physical strength to get him out of the situation if a problem occurred.

The only time he ventured out in Sikeston in a diminished capacity was to the high school basketball game to see my younger sister cheer. When we entered The Fieldhouse, a building that looks like a mini Astrodome, all eyes focused on Dad. As they recognized who he was, looks of shock came across their faces. Some people wept. They turned away, hoping to hide their reaction. As I pushed Dad in the wheelchair through the crowd, people patted him on the back, giving various expressions of love and appreciation. The unfolding scene represented what he wanted to avoid.

Dad had me stay to the side of the stands in the court's view but remaining as inconspicuous as possible. People who knew him sought us out to express their appreciation and condolences. I lost any shred of denial of his death at that moment because of this display of admiration. A few times, Dad had me take him behind the stands on the indoor track that circled the stadium. He was coughing, but I saw the outpouring of love had overwhelmed him. It filled me with pride while also breaking my heart. God was calling away someone who impacted so many beyond being my father.

During our family Christmas, Dad gave me his last enduring lesson of wisdom. He asked to be alone with me, where Dad told me the end was near. My father explained what was expected of me when he died. He didn't know if my older brother, stationed at a naval base in Japan, would make it back for his funeral, so Dad told me to support Mom planning it. It's a massive load to shoulder at nineteen, but I was ready and willing to take it on for him.

The conversation ended with something I will carry with me for the rest of my life. "Son, I have tried to teach you how to live like a man; now I will show you how to die like one."

April 9, 1986 – A Long Goodbye

Aunt Susan let me out at the front door of the Sikeston hospital. I race to Dad's room, hoping to get there before he dies. Despite making the four-hour trip in three hours, I have no way of knowing what I am walking into or if I made it in time. As I enter the room, a sense of relief calms me because he's alive. I made it! It yields way to the awareness I will witness my father's death.

My mood becomes an endless pit of sorrow when I learn Dad will never regain consciousness for us to utter; I love you one last time. It gnaws at my soul not knowing when we last spoke, did I say I love him? No matter how many times I tell him now throughout the night, it doesn't subdue my unease. I won't see the happiness in his eyes or hear him repeat those powerful words; I love you.

During the night with Mom, our prayers go from hopeful for some miraculous recovery to asking for Dad's release from his suffering. Did God even listen to our prayers, care what we wanted, or was He there? In those moments, I doubt Him.

Morning comes. He is still hanging on to life. Dr. Askew, Dad's close friend, makes his rounds and tells us it surprises him Dad is alive. He displays the most recent x-ray of Dad's lungs amazed how little lung capacity Dad has left. The doctor declares he's seen no one with this low level. He stuns me with his next statement, "Jeff, your father is the toughest man I have ever known." I immediately recall Dad foretelling of this moment at Christmas, "I will show you how to die like a man."

My emotions grow raw as the sleepless night weighs on me. It's not as heavy as my spirit. I know my world has only hours left with Dad. My paternal grandparents arrive along with my maternal grandparents, who bring my younger sister. We're gathered together for the last moments of my father's life.

Grandma Doris, Dad's mom, was in a horrendous car accident in the early 60s along with Grandpa Elza, my paternal grandfather. She suffered a traumatic brain injury so severe it wiped out her memory. Grandma relearned how to do everything. It made her reserved and detached but a kind woman during my life.

I witnessed a miraculous transformation in her when Dad, recovering from open lung surgery five years ago, called for his momma when she was in the room. Something connected in her mind that day as she became his momma again. More remarkable, it seemed to make her more linked with everyone. That is until today.

11

As we're in the last hour of Dad's life and the anticipation stress rises, it breaks Grandma Doris. She does a play-by-play of each breath taken by Dad, becoming the Howard Cosell of his death. With each breath, she says, "There's another one" or "He's still here." It wears on everyone. When Grandpa asks her to be quiet, nothing can distract her from this mental breakdown, not even when tempers flare. Mom and my sister scream at her to be silent or for Grandpa to take her out of the room. I become the referee to prevent the collapse of my family through this somber vigil.

After a while, things calm when Dr. Askew comes in for Dad's last moments. Grandma maintains her constant commentary. The room explodes with emotional sadness when Dad gives up his fight. I can't grieve at that moment since I need to support my family. Dr. Askew becomes concerned about my paternal grandfather's reaction, who backs himself into a corner wailing at the death of his only son. The doctor asks me to help soothe Grandpa Elza, so he doesn't have a heart attack.

Only with time and becoming a father, do I gain the appreciation for the crushing grief a parent losing a child must suffer. I am angry at being denied the time to mourn my dad's death the way I want.

The following days are a blur as we make funeral plans and a stream of visitors pay their respects. At the visitation, strangers tell stories about Dad and how he touched their lives. It comforts me. It also fuels my anger toward God. How could He remove an essential man from my life? My answer is there isn't a reason. I turn away from God, cutting off the roots of my faith.

August 1986 – The Fall

Pleased to be back at Ole Miss for my sophomore year, I hope it distracts from my immense heartache. I spent the summer building a large deck for our house. It's something Dad would have loved constructing with me. No matter how hard I hit the nails or how tired I made myself in the sweltering summer heat, the enormous pain didn't subside.

Moving into the fraternity house keeps me busy preparing my room for the upcoming year. Classes are starting in a few days, so the whole house is abuzz with activity. I must make my bed, which is a wood loft built the year before. Three steps up, the wooden ladder predictably slips out from under me on a wood floor.

"You dumbass," I think to myself between slipping and my backside hitting the floor.

My left leg goes between the rungs. I broke my leg; I believe since all my weight landed on the ladder. For a second, I assume I avoided significant injury when the limb is intact. Then the back, right side of my head throbs in pain as I feel considerable wetness pool around my motionless head. As I blackout, I realize my head hit the corner of a cinder block used to hold the door open.

My pounding head creates fogginess as I regain awareness. Uncertain how long I have been unconscious, I hear a different song piercing my ever-growing headache. I try to get up, but the room spins, giving me an appreciation for a boxer getting up from the canvas. After a few minutes, I grab the attention of my fraternity brothers who help contain the bleeding.

The severity of it becomes apparent when a squeamish housemate nearly passes out at the mere sight of me. I get several stitches at the emergency room and receive a diagnosis of a severe concussion. My frat brothers call my aunt, who picks me up from the hospital to stay at her house so she can keep an eye on me. The night is agonizing and nauseating, something I never experienced with concussions playing high school football. The headache is excruciating, and the room continually spins while I feel like I am on a boat caught in turbulent seas. I hope never to suffer anything like it again.

The next night, I find myself alone in a Holiday Inn room near downtown Oxford. It's a stupid decision on my part because my concussion-induced haze continues the unbearable headache, which also affects my balance.

This unwelcome solitude forces me to confront both the spiritual and physical pain engulfing my life. Why have you forsaken me and abandoned me, God? Why have you allowed so much agony in my life? I am broken! You can't be good to let this happen, so I don't need God in my life if You exist. I hate YOU! I am lost in the darkness of my soul.

Summer 1987 –Unwelcome News

Lounging on the couch, watching the evening news gives me some familiar comfort of my childhood when Dad would watch to keep abreast events. At the end of my summer break and not interested in what's happening, I half-listen. That is until I hear two words, pulmonary fibrosis, the disease that killed Dad unraveling my life.

I become laser-focused as the anchor announces the FDA approved a double lung transplant as a treatment for the disease. It significantly increases someone's lifespan. It's a knife to my heart not only because it's too late to save Dad, but they also denied him entry into the clinical trial. The trial excluded anyone over the arbitrary maximum age of forty, which Dad missed by two years. Anger builds imagining what could have been. My heart hardens further against God since I believe in my depths. He is responsible.

August 1991 – The Darkest Hour

Lost in a wilderness of despair, I consider the events of the last few weeks. I reached the depths of sad loneliness never even conceived of in my worst nightmares. Only two weeks before, my family traveled here for my wedding. I was in my tuxedo when the call came. The girl I was marrying disappeared. My bride told her family that the marriage was off before she left. The happiest day suddenly turned into a horrendous one.

Embarrassment exceeded the heartbreak because I was unmasked in front of my family who traveled from across the country, which created guilt over their expense. It's especially true for my brother, who was going to my best man, and his family because he's stationed in San Diego. My family showered me with love and support, but I wanted to run away and hide. It didn't ease the massive pain I felt.

Now, reliving the monumental shock, I fall into a pit of self-pity. All the perceived problems I endured these last years make me empty and rudderless. I agonize in shame since the hardships I have are nothing compared to others. The humiliation, guilt, heartbreak, grief, and isolation compound my spiritual parting from God.

The pain swamps my soul in torrential seas. Is life worth living? I devise ways to do the unthinkable to put an end to my miserable existence. I go as far as pulling out my rifle and chambering a shell.

It's in this moment of weakness I find strength from my upbringing founded in love and my Christian faith. I cry out for God's help to rescue me from this pitiful state. Give me something, God! At that instant with the loaded rifle across my lap, the phone rings breaking the madness of hopelessness.

My brother is checking-in to see how I am doing. He doesn't realize the God-given timing of his call because it breaks the unspeakable path I headed down. My brother senses my troubles and reassures that my best days are ahead. He tells me, I am loved. I don't retreat further into the darkness to permanently become lost.

Why the Darkness?

I chose darkness because I was mad at God. It seemed easier to hide there than confronting the reality of pain and sorrow in my life. It felt safer in the dark's numbness, so I convinced myself detachment from family, friends, and God was better. Retreating from life became my mantra. I filled the void within my soul with negative things like food, alcohol, and misguided relationships.

I never strayed too far, causing permanent damage. A solid foundation laid by my parents, family, and my hometown was a blessing. Church, teachers and my friend's parents helped develop my footings. Others lack the bedrock of parents, family, or community. When lost in darkness, it causes permanent damage.

Had I allowed myself to lean on the love of family and trusted God's love for me, I would have found the comfort I craved. Society teaches us to hide our pain and disguise our shame. Otherwise, it brands us with a scarlet letter. Instead, during these times of weakness, we should lean on others and God. When we are strong, we should become a comforting shoulder for someone to lean on with love and acceptance.

Out of the night that covers me,
Black as the pit from pole to pole,
I thank whatever gods may be
For my unconquerable soul.

William Ernest Henley from Invictus, the first stanza

1

DESCENDING INTO THE VALLEY OF DEATH

The Lord is my shepherd; I shall not want. He maketh me to lie down in green pastures: he leadeth me beside the still waters. He restoreth my soul: he leadeth me in the paths of righteousness for his name's sake.

Psalm 23: 1-3 (KJV)

When you're in your mid-twenties you understand you're not invincible like most teenagers believe they are. However, you imagine you're still immune to the health problems that seem to ravage people your parent's age in their forties and fifties. You spend most of your time trying to figure out how to be an adult.

Recently, I experienced a strange weakness in my left hand. When someone said it sounds like a pinched nerve, I assume a doctor can easily find a solution. Since I left for college, I visited nothing close to a regular doctor. Instead, I relied on university health clinics. This time is different because I am no longer a student, and Mom moved away from my family's hometown. A health issue and disconnection from where you consider home is upsetting.

I felt adrift for quite a while despite living in Springfield for five years since transferring from Ole Miss to Southwest Missouri State. I chose a health clinic near my work, but I don't think it provides much in the way of quality care. They herd everyone like cattle through their system. I saw a distracted and harried doctor. He squeezed my left arm, then my right for comparison, made me do a few movements with the left arm followed with several dismissive questions. I questioned myself for coming in and wasting his time. The doctor declared nothing was wrong. He said I'm out of shape and overweight, so I should work out. I already knew that! As he left, he added routinely, come back if this problem persists or gets worse.

I retreated from his office with my tail between my legs, assuming I did something wrong but determined to better my health. Even with the busy holiday season for retail sales, I rejoined a gym, lost weight, and sought alternative treatments like chiropractic care. It made sense getting in better shape and getting my back cracked would correct the problem if it's a pinched nerve.

I stopped focusing on the difficulties because of my efforts to reverse them. I questioned God what's happening even though my spirit still rejected Him for abandoning my life. It confused me as the weakness continued to spread. I grew tired. With the new year of 1993, I returned to the doctor who rejected my concerns. I missed the comfort of my childhood family doctors.

The choice to revisit the same disinterested doctor wasn't ideal. Starting over was a worse option. Since I recognized something was wrong, I realized he would send me on to a specialist. When I explained the spreading weakness as well as additional symptoms, cramps and weird twitching, the doctor became attentive. Within a few minutes, I went from expecting another blow-off to being referred to a neurologist which is ironically unnerving.

Another month passes before the neurologist appointment. The slow pace frustrates me oblivious to the potential seriousness of the problem. That changed once I saw the neurologist. He explained the symptoms are severe enough; the simplest explanation would require neck surgery to correct. The possibility freaked me out. He revealed a more critical condition like a brain tumor or Multiple Sclerosis (MS) were possibilities. Those words put the fear of God in you. They put you on notice that serious trouble is on the horizon:

It is distressing when you have turned your back on God. I was alone dealing with this since my family all lived far away, and I chose not to bother them. There was no reason to alarm them unnecessarily until I knew it was critical. Loneliness in a personal crisis makes the emotional burden you bear heavier, especially when you're lost in darkness. I felt abandoned and exposed.

Complex, painful procedures from blood work to an MRI to a spinal tap are how I spent the spring of 1993. I became accustomed to regular medical exams with the neurologist, which isn't comforting. At the final appointment, he had no answers. However, he believed my condition was acute enough to send my case to the MDA Neuromuscular Clinic at Barnes Hospital in St. Louis. It was becoming difficult to follow the sage lessons of my grandparents not to borrow trouble.

As I traveled up I-44 from Springfield to St. Louis, I began the journey back to God. It was a bumpy ride.

I started the discussion with, "God, it's been a while, you know why. If you're around, could you give me a break, and this is nothing?" The clouds didn't part. I heard no booming voice in response. I kept driving alone only listening to the rhythmic beat of the road passing rapidly beneath me. Ignored, yet again, I flipped on the radio and discovered one of my favorite tunes playing which I needed. I turned it up and let my spirit forget the conversation and why this trip was necessary. Bon Jovi always works.

As I pulled into Barnes, I realized my family lived near there when I was born while Dad finished dental school at Washington University. I recalled my parents showing where we lived during a trip to St. Louis. It flooded back comforting me in the distressing moment. After enduring another waiting area, I saw a neurologist who informed me nothing was wrong. His opinion, I was an anxious person who hyperventilated causing my issues. Anger welled up in me as he attempted to prove his point. He had me breathe fast into a brown paper bag to induce muscle twitches. The least concerning symptom had become the focus of this horse's ass. Later, I discovered spasms are a key symptom. His opinion was firm and dismissive, so it was fruitless to pursue anything further. It's not anxiety or hyperventilation.

After my correct diagnosis and being sent to the MDA clinic again, I determined it was the free community neurologic clinic, not the MDA clinic. They're the same office with different waiting rooms.

October 1, 1993 – Neurologist's Waiting Area

Sitting in a doctor's waiting room is strange. I endured fifteen waiting areas this past year, making me an expert. When you're in a condition needing care, you dread it. Everybody suffering a crisis expects something unpleasant awaits behind the next door creating an apprehensive setting. Standard stuff like physicals trigger images of painful procedures. You speculate on your exposure to nasty germs sitting there, and you sense the troubles of everyone. You know they're curious why you're here.

A waiting room stifles most conversations except for the occasional greetings. Sneezes, sniffles, and coughs or a child's cry in the distant exam room pierce the veil of silence. It's unsettling. When friends chat, they talk in hushed tones to not disturb the melancholy atmosphere. Funerals are festive in comparison. Relief from the quiet comes when the nurse calls someone. If it's not your name, at least your escape from this purgatory is closer.

I find myself in this painful situation yet again. It differs from a typical doctor's office because it is for a neurologist. People here are confronting cruel conditions. This practice is for a leading neurologist in St. Louis. My neurologist in Springfield referred me to him after the Barnes incident and further deterioration. This waiting room feels more ominous than any other during my near twenty-seven years. I hope things improve for my birthday later in October.

Everyone here is somber. I see an older gentleman in a wheelchair who looks emaciated like prisoners in Nazi concentration camps. I regret going to this appointment alone. Could I end up with anything close to that poor guy? Bless his soul as Granny B, my maternal grandmother, would say.

A week ago, I came here for the initial tests. It didn't seem as grave because my girlfriend, Lisa, was with me. After our vacation in San Diego a month ago, I plan to ask her to marry me once they figure out what's causing my symptoms. The tests appointment included an EMG and nerve conduction study, a painful experience. That visit wasn't awful and provided special moments. I introduced Lisa to Mom and my stepdad, Tom Weiskircher, when we stayed at their house. They recently moved to the St. Louis area from Rockford, Illinois. We even toured Washington University, where I applied for entrance into their prestigious MBA program. Those tests seem like a lifetime ago!

After my wedding disaster, I started a new job managing a computer and gaming store in the Battlefield Mall in Springfield. Bruised from my rejection, I threw myself into turning a brand-new store into one of the best performers in the country within months. I started to create new friends with people working in the surrounding stores. During slow days, we would chat at the front of our stores in the hallway.

One cute brunette worked at the shoe store next to me. We plunged into a routine of friendly conversations that would often continue the same topic over days. Everyone but me knew we would inevitably date. I took over six months to reach this realization myself and ask Lisa out for our first date in early 1992.

I can't believe the events over the last year that led me to this defining, terrible moment of truth. What started as some weakness in my left hand spread to other parts of my body.

The weird weakness created comical incidents such as once going to Lisa's place. As I walked into her apartment, my left hand strangely dropped the two-liter bottle of soda which exploded shooting like a rocket across the parking lot. The highlight of the episode, some guy at the pool yelled, "Whoa Dude! That was gnarly!" You can't help roaring with laughter at that moment even when there's cause for concern.

There were troubling incidences too like when on a break from Babbage's in the Battlefield Mall, I fell walking to the food court. I didn't trip on anything prompting the stumble and fall. My legs stopped working, causing me to face plant onto the unforgiving concrete floor bloodying my nose. I laid there, stunned and embarrassed by what happened. In my mind, I looked like a beached gray whale at six feet two inches, two hundred seventy-five pounds in a gray suit. Concern and confusion built as falls and other issues happened with alarming frequency. Eight years earlier, I was at my physical peak. I played football and wrestled for Sikeston High School. Only a decade ago, I hiked one-hundred and ten miles in the Rockies of New Mexico at Philmont Scout Ranch. Still young, I lay in the hallway throbbing in pain as the cold concrete penetrated my agony. I couldn't comprehend my sudden physical struggles.

I remember thinking then like now as I'm waiting for my test results, why was my life interrupted by these physical challenges? WHY GOD?

My Temple of Doom

Awakened from my thoughts with the declaration "Jeffrey Lester," I stand giving the obligatory hand raise showing here. Before disappearing behind the portal of my unknown destiny, I glance over toward the older gentleman slumping in the wheelchair. He catches my gaze and gives me a reassuring smile despite the suffering he must go through. Please don't let me have anything close to what he has, I think. The nurse escorts me to the chamber of doom. She says as she seals me in, "The doctor will be in shortly."

Seconds seem like hours. The ticking second hand of the clock breaks the stillness counting down the end of my existence. I want to be anywhere, but here. A sense of dread has me in its grips and won't let go. My inner child screams to run and hide from my future. The walls close in sealing me in this tomb. I jump as the door cracks open, startling me out of my fears of what's happening.

"How are you doing Mr. Lester?" the doctor utters as we exchange pleasantries. The doctor has been cordial during my visits. A noticeable change in mood occurs as he looks at my file, which is frightening. An excruciating amount of time passes before he takes a deep breath and looks in my eyes. "Mister Lester, there is no easy way to tell you this, but you have Amyotrophic Lateral Sclerosis, ALS, or commonly known as Lou Gehrig's Disease."

What? I am unsure if I mutter a word as I emotionally detach with each sentence of explanation of what ALS is. He explains the total disability I will experience before I succumb to the disease, dying in three to five years. The one clear thing he advises me to do is plan my funeral, "You know, have a big party before you die." No potential treatment, no alternatives just plan my funeral? NO HOPE!!!

Leaving the doctor's office, I'm void of emotion or awareness of anything around me. It's through God's grace and the angels guiding me that I survive the drive through highway traffic to Mom's house.

The truth of this drastic turn my life took doesn't hit me until I walk into the house and see my mother. Like a massive tidal wave, the realities of my new life wipe out all my old plans, hopes, and dreams in that horrific instant as emotions wash over me. All of it must be visible in my physical appearance as it strips my soul bare for all to see. The distress in Mom's voice as she asks me what's wrong reflects my overwhelming desperation and grief of loss. The moment I utter the words, "I have ALS," the weight of the reality crushes me wailing onto the floor. After that point, I am a dead man walking through the valley of the shadow of death.

Yea, though I walk through the valley of the shadow of death, I will fear no evil: for thou art with me; thy rod and thy staff they comfort me. Thou preparest a table before me in the presence of mine enemies: thou anointest my head with oil; my cup runneth over.
Surely goodness and mercy shall follow me all the days of my life: and I will dwell in the house of the Lord forever.

Psalm 23: 4-6 (KJV)

2

FINDING THE LIGHT IN MY DARKNESS

Two roads diverged in a wood, and
I took the one less traveled by,
And that has made all the difference.

Robert Frost from The Road Not Taken

Sometimes in life, what seems trivial to the rest of the world helps decide what direction your life takes. I am at that point where I accept my fate and choose the quick road to death or choose the uncertain path to living life on my terms.

Before January 1994, three words change, confusion, and anger define the months since my ALS diagnosis. Change seized all aspects of my life. My deterioration compelled uprooting my life in Springfield to move nearby family, expecting my physical decline and needs. I transferred my job with Babbages to manage stores in the St. Louis area.

Prior to moving, I fractured my leg above the ankle. It's a preview of the physical dependence on others I will later experience since I'm unable to move myself. It foreshadows what becomes the most challenging part of life with ALS, dependence.

I live with my mom and Tom at first. After several weeks, I move into a second-story apartment in Clayton, Missouri, with my younger sister, Laura who was also living at Mom's house. I don't want to spend my last independent days living with my parents. I notice further weakness, but I don't grasp the rapid physical decline coming as evidenced by choice of residence.

The confusion comes from what's happening because of ALS and what remains of my life. There's limited information about ALS. Dire predictions come from my doctors who tell me to give up and die. Then there is information about Lou Gehrig's Disease from the Muscular Dystrophy Association (MDA) and a newer organization, the ALS Association. They paint bleak pictures of life with ALS. However, they provide some hope with planning for future changes and support. I receive some sparse info from other ALS patients met at clinics and support groups about the possibility of building a life beyond ALS. All these different realities confuse me.

Unwanted opinions from family and friends about living or dying annoy me because they project their views and fears of life onto my decision. During Thanksgiving and Christmas, I see pity in everyone's eyes, making me want to scream, "I am still here, I'm still alive!"

Anger with a big dose of sadness dominates my emotions when I allow myself to feel anything. The full holiday season for a retail store manager along with two moves gives an illusion of busyness deceiving my brain into not confronting reality. My impending death hangs over my head like the freshly sharpened blade of a guillotine.

The numbness created in my mind and spirit frees me from my normally rational and sound decisions. Why should I care because I am dying soon?

I continue a relationship with my girlfriend, Lisa, who lives in Springfield, which is who my heart desires while accepting dates with other women. Confused by my impending death, anger haunts my soul. Whenever I'm alone, the demons of my situation overcome me. The disdain toward my body and God surpasses my desire for His help to save me from ALS and myself.

Lisa moves to St. Louis in January to give support. It's my madness that forces me to push her away by breaking up. How can I love anyone when doctors claim my life's over? Sometimes God protects us when we're fools!

I'm alone in my room searching for answers on the internet, whatever that is. Someone told me I could talk to other people with ALS on it. It's a forum on a website called Prodigy. It's a revelation to get real feedback about my condition if I find people with ALS. I load the software on my personal computer with great anticipation of a breakthrough. A better understanding of Lou Gehrig's Disease can pull me out of the limbo between living and death, where I find myself.

I get through the usual setup screens when the program asks me for a username. This is my identification on the forum. It also serves as my address for electronic mail. Whatever that useless thing is. The program explains it should not be any version of your name, but something unique describing who you are or your beliefs. For most people, the question doesn't register beyond a moment of amusement trying to create a clever or funny name. For me, who's in an identity crisis because ALS wiped out everything, it's a crucial question about how I live the rest of my life.

The question hits me like a freight train. It rips off the bandage of numbness, exposing the incredible pain buried deep in my soul. I weep and mourn the life I lost, deserved. ALS denied the hope of a wife, children, career, or anything as it drove my life into a ditch. Based on what's coming, I won't exit this ditch. I ask God for release from that burden so allowing me to move forward with the remnants of my life toward better days.

After a while, my attention turns back to the computer, where the question remains unanswered with flashing cursor pleading for a response. The decision might be inconsequential, but now I am using my answer as a shining beacon to guide my life's journey. My parents raised me to create my path. This guide means not giving into ALS and its disability. Accepting my fate means an agonizing, meaningless march to death before I am thirty. It's not what Dad did. I won't give up and die either. He fought tenaciously to build his life and live it on his terms, so following Dad's example, that's what I will do. The strength of this realization pulls me out of the funk of despair, where I have resided since my diagnosis. It frees my soul.

I pace like a caged animal. Although it's only a silly name, it gives me the strong push needed to move ahead with my life. This username must be right. God help me find this word. After thinking through and rejecting various ideas, animals come to mind. Native Americans choose names based on representative spirit animals. What do I want my spirit animal to be?

I want something that conveys physical strength and power since ALS is taking mine away. Lion, elephant, tiger, all come to mind, but they seem too exotic for this purpose. Bear enters my thoughts, yes, that's it! I saw bears roaming in the wild when I hiked one-hundred-ten miles in the Rockies of New Mexico at Philmont Scout Ranch. Bear works, but it doesn't express how I want to fight ALS.

Conversations with God continue until I discover my username. Quite satisfied, I type Ragingbear, tenacious strength despite my weakness. For now, I don't fully understand what this means, but moving forward, it's how I will live with ALS!

February 1994 – Rebuilding Begins

I spend most my spare time on the Prodigy ALS forum, absorbing whatever experience and knowledge I can glean from those willing to share their experiences with ALS. I realize there are two distinct groups of thought. One side, where I had been since my diagnosis is a dark, hopeless place where people lament their destroyed lives. They wallow in bitterness, awaiting their demise. I understand their attitudes and see the appeal of living in hopelessness. I don't want to live there anymore.

The other group of people is positive about living their lives with ALS despite being more advanced in their progression. It's counter to the picture painted by the medical professionals involved in my care. The scenarios are contrary to everything I learned before. It's hard to entertain hope for a life outside of this death march.

I start slowly trust there's a chance to rebuild my shattered life into a life worth living. It's remarkably different from what I planned before ALS entered my life, but my heart tells me it's worth pursuing. As hard as their lives seem, the people I met on the forum appear to have happy and fulfilling lives filled with love.

I ponder these new possibilities while driving back to our apartment after visiting Mom and Tom with my younger sister, Laura. It's a thirty-minute drive providing ample opportunity to steer the conversation to my dilemma. I explain what I learned from the ALS forum and how I want to take back my life from Lou Gehrig's

Disease. The conversation morphs into a discussion about my relationship with my ex-girlfriend, Lisa. It weighs on my heart.

When Laura asks, "What about Lisa?" I blurt out everything I desire, including if not for ALS, I would ask her to marry me. Laura thoughtfully listens to my problems. Then I ask her the burning question I struggle with since my diagnosis, "How do I pull Lisa into the hell I am facing if I love her?" She stares ahead as she forms her well-reasoned response. Laura turns and says, "Don't you think Lisa should be the one to decide that?"

As straightforward as this question is, it's a bolt of lightning that jolts me awake. I became so preoccupied with myself, adrift in the raging seas of ALS, I lost sight of anything good in my life. I eliminated the best part of my life, Lisa. At that moment, an epiphany strikes me.

Live your life not based on your troubles instead focus on the positives in your life, which is the key to unlocking happiness.

February 19, 1994 – The First Step

Even with my diagnosis of a fatal, disabling disease at this point, its primary impact is the emotional destruction of my life. Physically, outside of some clumsiness, I feel healthy even though I know devastating changes are brewing inside. It might be a blessing since I was able to get back on my feet again emotionally and spiritually without dealing with significant physical changes.

My turmoil wasted precious time, especially with Lisa. I now realize living in regret over past mistakes does nothing for your current happiness. I try valuing each day with love. It's why I'm sitting in front of Lisa's apartment for the first date on what I hope will be the rest of our lives together.

I pray Lisa can forgive my mistakes and the sheer stupidity I showed in the last months. God give me a chance to prove my love to her again. She doesn't understand the torment I endured.

The doctor's declaration that my life was over caused me to shut out everyone from my struggles. The person I needed most wasn't there because I allowed medical predictions and other people's opinions about my life control my actions instead of following my heart. I hope she sees past these blunders to recognize my love giving us a chance to create a life together. I shut my car door, taking the first step toward my hopeful future.

May 1994 – Yes and Oh No

The past few months are heaven in my eyes. Lisa and I resumed our relationship, which grew closer and stronger. During this time, I experienced the bliss of regular romantic life. It's my last moments of normalcy, so I savor each of them creating lasting memories.

Funny moments like when I grabbed a thigh master as a weapon against a potential intruder are special. After discovering it was nothing, Lisa and Laura had a good laugh at my expense. Mundane tasks like taking a flight of stairs are meaningful because it's normal even as it becomes harder reminding me change is lurking.

The only reminder of what lies ahead is meeting with a social worker from the ALS Association at our apartment with Lisa and Laura. I arranged it for Lisa's benefit. She needs all the information possible about our potential future. I know most of the information she told us.

Hearing the details of how ALS will dismantle my body, making me dependent on others for even the most basic things taken for granted was upsetting and unsettling. I cannot imagine how it hit Lisa, but later, when we were alone, she tells me she loves me, and

WE will face whatever is ahead as one. God blessed me with an unbelievable woman of strength and beauty that's full of love. Together we can overcome anything.

I let everything set in before asking Lisa to marry me. She says YES and in doing so she pulls my life out of the ditch ALS put it into back in October. I float in a dream instead of planning the empty celebration of a life that didn't happen. I am living the life I am supposed to live. This happiness allows me to ignore my worsening foot drag and gait.

My attention remains distracted from ALS issues, so today, my only concern is hurrying off to work. I rush out the door, putting my suit coat on as I reach the top of the stairs. My foot drags snagging the rubber lip that covers the edge of the stair, sending me hurtling in the air over the ten steps. The flight stops when I plow headfirst into the cinder block wall of the landing between the floors. It's a hard way to learn that ALS and stairs aren't a good combination.

Stubbornness and desire to live a normal life means I don't learn the lesson. The event sets in motion the urgent need to move again in June. That August, I'm forced on disability by Babbages.

In the fell clutch of circumstance
I have not winced nor cried aloud.
Under the bludgeonings of chance
My head is bloody, but unbowed.

William Ernest Henley from Invictus, the second stanza

3

A SOLID FOUNDATION

If you have built castles in the air, your work need not be lost; that is where they should be. Now put the foundations under them.

Henry David Thoreau from Walden

When given the opportunity to rebuild my life, I focused on building a solid foundation from what I mourned and desired most from the life I lost: a wife, family, and love.

The gravest symptoms of ALS elude my everyday reality except for being forced on disability. Exhaustion prevented working on some scheduled days, so my failure to keep assignments forced the inevitable. My illness wouldn't allow employment even though I hoped to keep working. Fortunately, with my brother's recent retirement from the Navy and with our mom and stepdad's backing, he opened a Minuteman Press in Chesterfield. Lisa and I live nearby.

I offered to help Greg get things up and running since I have business and computer experience. It keeps me somewhat busy otherwise, I would drive Lisa crazy, sticking my nose into the wedding plans. She threw me a bone putting me in charge of the music. No wedding's music was so thoroughly planned. There's an unspoken harsh truth of ALS coming, boredom and feeling useless. I haven't fully seen this reality yet, but the glimpses I experienced are upsetting.

It's a week before our wedding date on October 8th meaning today is the first anniversary of my ALS diagnosis. I'm in a somber mood despite the positive changes taking place that allowed me to seize back my life from ALS. I don't fully appreciate that God blesses me beyond imagination, including in ways Jesus teaches us to not worry about food, clothes, or shelter.

It's the six-month window before my long-term disability income kicks in. My vacation hours ran out, so the problematic financial realities of ALS started. The only reason it doesn't produce devastation is the good fortune of living in the same apartment building as my cousin, Shelby. Without this twist of fate, our contact would be sparse. He's in the financial field and recommended a company who buys life insurance which I had through Babbages. They purchased my policy and will deposit the money by November. They're gambling on my death before their venture turns negative, but I hope to outlive their speculation on my grave. I don't know if I will win this race, but either way, the money is coming when it's needed averting a severe financial crisis.

It's been a journey getting to our wedding. While the future is uncertain, I plan on taking in everything that day with a joyful spirit. For months I lived a stark, unfulfilling life without Lisa in it. A hollow existence void of happiness, love, or expectation of better days ahead isn't a life I wish to live.

The wedding occurs in the First United Methodist Church in Lisa's hometown of Lebanon, Missouri. We don't realize this church and this town will play a central and vital role in the family life, Lisa and I are creating. I cannot imagine a world without Lisa in it. Thank God He guided me on a path making her my wife.

Lisa has been out at the store getting dinner, which I usually enjoy doing with her, but today I was too tired. She doesn't realize today marks the anniversary of my ALS diagnosis since I didn't mention it. I guess she is wrapped up in wedding mode which is fine since I don't want to discuss it. When she gets back, Lisa disappears into our bedroom for a while before coming out and sitting by me on the couch. She tells me we got a special gift today. I assume it's another wedding present which has been streaming in with the wedding next week.

Something is different because she is smiling at me with a mischievous grin. Now I'm curious, "What is it?" As she pulls something out to show me, she says, "I am pregnant!" Joy overwhelms me since this is beyond anything that I dreamed possible one year ago when experiencing painful life-ending news. How different and blessed my life became after doctors declared it over. God gave me extra innings in my Game of Life.

April 1995 – Face Planting

I dropped Lisa off at St. John's office complex in Creve Coeur for her doctor's appointment. Since it's close by, I run a quick errand for Minuteman picking up software at CompUSA which is two exits north on I-270. I reckon there's plenty of time to do it before she's called back, but I need to hustle to see the latest pictures of my beautiful daughter. Besides, it's one less waiting room to endure. I spend enough time in them. I am surprised they aren't charging me rent.

My getting to this point where I am a husband and father seemed an impossible prospect when beginning my journey with Lou Gehrig's Disease. Now I am living a fantasy within the nightmare of ALS. I realize how important life is beyond the physical realm, where many people exist. There are still more challenging losses coming soon. The growing struggles I already experience gives me the outlook to love and value the unique moments each day provides.

It's exciting to view our child forming in Lisa. I cried when my daughter kicked my hand. As joyous as it was when Lisa told me she was pregnant, I had serious doubts I would live to meet my child. When given a death sentence, it lessens your expectations. Only within the last month did I allow myself to believe I could live to see and hold my precious daughter. We finally settled on the name Kelsey. I didn't realize naming your child would be such a debate, but it's one of the joyful times I am happy I experienced.

Lost in the thoughts of becoming a dad, I make the quick drive up to the computer store. It's heavenly envisioning our little girl in our lives. The strange sensation of being full of joy while wondering how long you will live around becomes a constant state for me. Will I impact Kelsey's life in any significant way? I cannot help but let a passing thought of sadness enter my happy world. It's in those moments; I learn to not fixate on the tragic parts of life or the potential storms on the horizon. I narrow my focus to the positive elements of my life appreciating each day.

My head swirls with these thoughts as I struggle to get out of my car and hurry into the store. In a rush, I don't recognize the lip on the wheelchair ramp leading into the store. My foot drags, causing me to fall. This time when my brain tells my arms to brace for the fall, they remain by my sides, making me face plant into the sidewalk. I turn my head just before hitting, which avoids a devastating blow to my face. I can hear my brother saying it would have been an improvement!

Stunned for a moment, I discover I cannot get myself up into a sitting position. I labor doing more tasks lately, but this is beyond that. Maybe I am more hurt than I realize. The only things bothering me are a scraped cheek and my throbbing, bloody nose. Panic overtakes me as people gather to help. An ambulance is called. I recognize, for the first time, ALS rendered me helpless. The paramedic checks me, but I refuse treatment. It would reveal I was powerless. Instead, I can tell Lisa I fell, maintaining my facade of independence.

September 1995 – Pantsed by ALS

Everything is well with our tiny family, and Kelsey is doing terrific. She sprouts to a new level each day while I continue to wither away. ALS is taking a noticeable toll on my body. Walking is becoming an obvious problem as I toil with each step. Someone might think I am drunk or realize I'm disabled because my gait is unsteady. My legs drag a step behind where my brain believes they should be. It seems like ALS strapped weights to my wrists, making my arms dangle lifelessly at my sides when I walk. For those who think I might be drunk, my slurred speech reinforces their suspicion.

Aware of people's reactions, I tell people my issues are from ALS. It elicits the response, *What's that?* I find out the easiest way people understand is saying it's a disease covered by the Jerry Lewis MDA Telethon on Labor Day. One quick older gentleman had the best response. He smiled saying, "You're a little old to be one of Jerry's Kids." He got that the disease does not define me.

My weight drops at an alarming rate from the same issue, which is causing my speech to slur. Someone on the ALS forum joked that ALS is the best diet ever.

I realize dressing to go to Dierberg's with Lisa; my shorts are bunching up. I tighten the belt to compensate for the fifty pounds lost. I hesitate to buy new ones because at this rate there are several sizes and another fifty pounds before hitting my ideal weight of one-hundred and ninety. It's a waste buying something that fits for only a month or two.

Dierberg's is a high-end grocery store near our apartment. One of our favorite date nights is wandering through the store finding special treats, renting a movie, and snuggling on the couch. Lisa likes to call herself a cheap date. One thing I love most about her; she appreciates the moments we have together more than what we are doing. It's something I'm keenly aware of recognizing this window of relative normalcy is closing.

When we enter the store, I grab a cart per our usual routine. Anymore it's a safety net for my unsteadiness. We're doing more than our regular date night of casual shopping since my parents are keeping Kelsey for the night. We might as well kill two birds with one stone. Lisa has her list checking things off as we go, which is a change from my guy way of shopping, rambling around the store hungry, seeing what catches my fancy.

There's one thought on my mind tonight, chocolate covered macaroons from the bakery. It's my favorite treat.

I become Lisa's errand boy gathering nearby items to check off her master list. Most times, I take the cart along with me. One last request to fetch something forgotten in the frozen food aisle, I leave the safety of the cart with Lisa in the dairy section. She will need it more.

I wobble off on my last mission with my mind set on the delicacy of macaroons. They're secure in the cart's seat to avoid being crushed. As I turn down the aisle, my shorts fall. I catch and pull them up. Boy, that would have been embarrassing! Halfway down the aisle, my shorts fall again only this time I barely grab them with two right fingers. I am in a real pickle now because, in my current state of physical instability, I will tumble over bending over to pull my shorts up. The last thing I want is to be sprawled on the floor hearing, "Pickup on aisle four."

I lean against the freezer, assuring my balance. Seconds passing seem like minutes as I consider my predicament and what to do. The saving grace in this utterly embarrassing moment is my untucked shirt is longer because of my recent weight loss. At least I'm not standing here in the glory of my tighty-whities.

The other saving grace, the store is empty. I realize after several attempts at a yell whisper for Lisa that it's also a curse. I am chilled and shivering on my way to becoming a popsicle. It causes my fingers to release my shorts, dropping the last shreds of imagined dignity to my ankles. One person has ventured down the aisle. They didn't notice there was a problem. If they had, I would have surely heard "Security! Pervert on aisle four!"

Now grasping my dilemma, I need help from anyone. A woman stocking the shelves notices my distress. Any humiliation leaves my thoughts since I want my shorts up to hasten my escape from this arctic tundra. I ask her to get my wife because I need help. After a brief explanation of where Lisa is and what she looks like, my angel of mercy hurries away finding Lisa to rescue me. No one ever told me ALS could pants you!

February 1996 – A Final Fall

I fight to maintain my independence, trying to convince my family I'm not growing weaker and more helpless daily. The reality is I'm fooling myself. Since my fall at CompUSA, it numbered my days living as a self-sufficient man.

Today was brutal on the ALS front. I agreed to fix a computer issue for Greg at the print shop, but I woke up exhausted. I put off going out. Fatigue frequently happens these days. It's a fight to do anything because ALS is assaulting my breathing muscles. Lisa helps more even for routine tasks such as putting on socks. The physical changes are piling up and taking their toll on me.

The big bright spot in my life is the time spent with Lisa and Kelsey. It's an unexpected blessing from ALS since I get more time with them. If I could work, I would miss many special moments, especially with Kelsey, who changes every day.

Our dinner routine is a wonderful time, so I put off fixing the computer until tonight. Every night at dinner, I use a lap tray in my La-Z-Boy because it's easier eating there than at the table. I prop my elbows on the tray, shortening the distance for my arms to feed myself. A mundane task most people take for granted becomes a harder struggle for me every day. My arms feel like increasingly heavier weights are on them.

Kelsey loves the arrangement. Each night she crawls to the couch then uses it to hand walk to my chair, smiling big, beginning our nightly dance. Once Kelsey gets to the tray, she reaches for my food and sweet tea giggling as I repeat no with a smile. Kelsey recognizes she has Daddy wrapped around her finger getting whatever she wants.

After dinner, I kiss them goodbye and leave for the shop. It's dark and cold. Even realizing I am vulnerable if there's a problem, I'm determined to do things myself despite growing physical challenges. Two easy steps lead up to the parking lot from our apartment. They're more challenging to navigate recently. My foot catches taking the first stair causing me to trip. I grab the rail, stopping my fall. With my legs straddling the steps and the weakness of my upper body, I cannot recover to a standing position. I quickly understand it's inevitable I'm going to the ground so I lower myself to it as gracefully as I can.

After a few minutes with both feet on the apartment walkway, I hope I can muster enough power to pull myself up, saving the embarrassment of needing help. After multiple attempts, I don't have enough strength. I sit there hoping in this vast, busy apartment complex someone ventures by so they can assist.

After ten minutes, no one comes around. I become chilled; there's no choice but to call out. With my diminishing lung capacity, I don't have enough volume to yell.

"Help!" No response. "Help!!!" No response. "Someone, please HELP!" No response. I'm getting cold and shivering after another ten minutes, about twenty-five minutes total. My voice is getting weaker.

I see the shadows of my neighbor and Kelsey and Lisa through the sliding glass doors on the decks about ten yards away from me. To add insult to injury, it starts snowing. A proverb comes to my mind, "Pride comes before a fall." Could this be how my life ends?

After thirty minutes, I say, "God, please help me." He was by my side the whole time patiently waiting because, within seconds, our neighbor comes out their door. They get Lisa, and together they assist me standing.

The self-reliant part of my life ended this day since I never go out alone again. It forces another move to a house that's made accessible for a power wheelchair. Soon I will use the wheelchair to go anywhere.

Beyond this place of wrath and tears
Looms but the Horror of the shade,
And yet the menace of the years
Finds, and shall find me, unafraid.

William Ernest Henley from Invictus, the third stanza

4

SEEING THE LIGHT

We can easily forgive a child who is afraid of the dark;
the real tragedy of life is when men are afraid of the light.

Plato

Since my fall in the winter of 1996, my family and progression are in a constant state of change. Before the fall, most modifications I could make myself offsetting my failing condition. It focused on walking and being aware of limits. Everything else was annoying and a struggle, but I only needed to make minor alterations maintaining the facade of a normal life. After falling, this wasn't the situation. It's like I fell off a cliff with changes coming in rapid succession. Any pause was me grabbing a ledge by my fingertips, providing a temporary delay praying God spares me from falling further.

I agreed not to go outside alone. Much harder to shoulder was when I quit driving. It's such a symbol of independence, manhood, and self-control I won't get over losing that capability. Bearing it is tough because in my mind it's the last vestige of my former life. It's the undeniable beginning of a life determined by my ever-growing list of disabilities.

An existence dependent on others is an unbearable load. Any scrap of freedom is like gold. Our family moves to a house adapted with a ramp so I can leave in my power wheelchair. It's the toughest emotional change for me to acknowledge as a husband and father, my disease dictates and limits the options of our family's life.

More annoying and exhausting is the relentless pace of continual changes we must compensate for in our lives. When we solve my inability to stand on my own, for instance, within weeks, we confront my inability to grasp a cup. We seek solutions for drinking without help. We're in a never-ending cycle of new problems and finding the best, least disruptive solution for our lives. The worst part is we know every change is a temporary fix with more daunting issues on the horizon.

A horse accident the day after Kelsey's birth paralyzed actor Christopher Reeve, aka Superman. I developed a kinship to his story because he instantly became a quadriplegic what I am slowly turning into because of ALS. I realize it's a blessing for us making a bunch of tiny steps toward his level of disability, but it's like a death from a thousand paper cuts. Sometimes I want it over with, so I can decide if I continue or how to move on with my life.

The ironic part about my fall into the dependency is it happens simultaneously with Kelsey developing from an infant to an adorable girl. It's another blessing God gives me. Instead of focusing on my losses, most days, I revel in seeing her grow up. As I need the wheelchair, I delight in Kelsey walking then running and jumping. As I struggle to move a computer mouse with my hand, I get pleasure watching Kelsey play games on my computer while sitting on my lap.

As my speech becomes unrecognizable to people, and it's challenging to eat, I see our precious daughter explore, learn, and expand her abilities. She discovers everything in this world with the wonder and joy only a child possesses. God uses her, teaching me to enjoy life's small gifts and moments since that's where real happiness lies.

Even in my perfect world with Lisa and Kelsey, I cannot resist the frustration and depression building up about my worsening condition. I recognize many awful limitations are coming. For a change of scenery, I asked Mom to take me to the family print shop. I need to escape the house and refresh my spirit that's swimming in a pool of negativity. It's nice chatting with Greg at the shop while Mom runs errands. The hours pass quick giving me a brief respite. It also reminds me of the life I'm missing so I go home more in a funk.

After Mom helps me out of the van, I drive my wheelchair into the garage where the wheelchair ramp into the house is located. I'm set to navigate up it when a wayward sparrow flies into the garage straight up Mom's dress. She lets out squeals of terror harkening back to her schoolgirl days. She dances around the garage like she's on hot coals. I about fall out of my chair, laughing so hard at the scene unfolding before my eyes. I cannot speak from laughing when Kelsey and Lisa burst out the door to the kitchen, curious about the commotion. Mom has a love-hate relationship with birds. Thank you, God! Whenever I'm down, I remember this lifting my spirit.

August 1997 – My World Closing In

Pulmonologist Visit

My sister is taking me to my appointment today. Despite hoping tests show nothing has changed from the last visit, I realize in my heart the news won't be positive. It's harder to breathe when lying in bed. It's like I'm continually jogging. The pulmonologist appointments are trying since the lung capacity tests are the same ones I remember Dad going through. A vivid childhood memory was on one of his appointments in Memphis, my crying when the nurse yelled at him.

For my respiratory appointment at the ALS MDA Clinic in Barnes, they put me in a booth, strap on a mouthpiece, and put on headphones for the therapist's instructions. It's different from Dad's test decades ago. Still, the given instructions are, "Big breath in and PUSH, PUSH, PUSH, PUSH," takes me right back to Dad. It makes me misty-eyed missing him.

On this appointment, my wheelchair must sit right by the booth where my sister and the therapist assist me getting into the box. It's a complicated three-way dance maneuver and a stark reminder of how far I degraded. It foretells my results.

My sister and I move to an exam room after they complete the test. The doctor comes in and flatly states I'm months away from respiratory failure. I already grasp it means death or choosing a trache and going on a ventilator. He asks if we have questions which I have none from the intimate knowledge gleaned from people on ventilators on the ALS forum. I understand, for this decision, doctors give profoundly misinformed opinions about life on ventilators. Even though I recognize Laura is champing at the bit to ask a million questions, she follows my lead.

Sensing my last opportunity for a public outing if I decide against venting, I ask Laura to visit the Crestwood Mall where I last worked. I realize for many; they would go somewhere new and exciting. I desired a familiar place when I was well. Laura pulls into a handicapped spot at the entrance I used when I worked there. It's busy for a weekday afternoon. We take the last remaining accessible parking spot in front of the mall entrance. I can't deny I'm disabled any longer.

It takes several minutes for her to figure out the lift situation since it's a recent addition. The lift won't unfold so while Laura and I try to figure out the problem, a cranky old man pulls up behind us and honks his horn. Laura pops her head out the van doorway and nicely informs him we're not leaving. He knew this because we were jockeying for spots. I only hear his muffled response, but I can tell he's cussing her out. She finally yells back, "Well yeah, but we're more handicapped than you!"

When Laura gets back in, as any good sibling would when given a prime opportunity to take a verbal shot, I say grinning, "Maybe mentally you are Sis!" We both needed the good laugh that followed washing the troubles of this day away.

A Movie Moment

Before Laura returns to DC, the whole family gathers at Mom and Tom's house for a Sunday dinner. Some of the family watches Field of Dreams. It's a terrific way to pass the time until we eat. That is until the *incident* happens. The emotional buildup during the whole movie for Ray to ask the ghost of his dad to play catch unleashes a torrent of crying. I call them ALS emotions. One of the lesser-known side effects of Lou Gehrig's Disease is the impact on a person's emotions. It doesn't matter whatever emotion I feel, happy to sad, anger to joy. If the emotional response is strong enough, it triggers an uncontrollably ugly cry.

A movie that pulls on the heartstrings starts me. Throw in that Field of Dreams is about a father and son, it's no surprise it causes one of my most intense episodes ever. Amid my crying, I don't realize my crying outburst is contagious to everyone. The ample bawling and commotion cause other family members to rush into the room to see what all the ruckus is. After everyone calms down from the cathartic crying session, it's hilarious when my brother and stepdad say they won't watch Field of Dreams with me again!

The Tragic Night

I tried sleeping in our bed tonight, but it's difficult to breathe when lying down since I must remind my body to take a breath, making sleep impossible to achieve. On nights like this, I find myself in my La-Z-Boy watching television all night, which makes breathing more comfortable. I hope I can sneak in a catnap or two. I have trouble using my thumb to change channels. Lisa sets it where I press one button to flip between two preferred channels.

I learned the hard way by attempting anything else. The remote slips and I get stuck watching something undesirable. It makes each second an agonizing as I wait for either Kelsey or Lisa to wake up and change the channel. It's terrible when Kelsey turning on her pre-school shows is a welcome relief. Tonight, one of the channels is a news channel which is on when the breaking news occurs. Princess Diana has been in an automobile accident in Paris.

They talk about the tragedies she endured and the now tragic end to her life. It's not lost on me that the end of my life is coming soon. It didn't matter that she was rich, famous, and adored by billions around the world; she experienced pain and sorrow. We all live through love's rejection in some form and face difficulties of our own making or someone else's. It tears us down, causing us to retreat into a bubble of loneliness and despair. We must decide if we remain there or if we utilize the God-given strength within us to pull ourselves out of our misery or use that strength to seek help when we cannot do it ourselves.

No matter if you're Princess Diana or someone like me battling a horrific, debilitating disease, we all have burdens to bear. Only we control the direction our lives take no matter how many storms batter it. I believe Diana found that strength to be happy and loved in the end. I pray I can summon that strength as I fight for my life in the coming months.

December 1997 – The End is Near?

December 17 – Saying Goodbye

Admitted to the hospital several days ago after awakening in the middle of the night gasping for breath, I couldn't pull in enough air. This started my possible last days. Strangling to death in Lou Gehrig's Disease's hands is not how I wish to meet my earthly demise. I woke Lisa to call an ambulance. My carbon dioxide levels were off the charts to the point a doctor commented that it amazed him I was conscious and held any conversation. He said I was equivalent to someone wasted.

They tried a new therapy for ALS, a bi-pap ventilator, which brought my levels down. However, they determined it wasn't enough. I either go on invasive trache ventilation or live less than two weeks. The grim reality of ALS has its cold hands around my throat, choking the life out of me.

Initially, I wanted to go home since I hadn't decided on what direction to take for this fork in my life's journey. I wasn't ready to confront my mortality. The months before were a never-ending run uphill growing steeper each day. Any activity, including eating, would stress and exhaust me. Sometimes I had to remind my body to breathe. During those months, I was existing, not living.

After discussions with Lisa based on knowledge gained from conversations with people who have ALS on ventilators, we chose the trache surgery.

We believe that's the end of deliberations. It wasn't. One pompous St. John's ICU doctor interjected himself into the well-reasoned and personal decision. He wove a story of how horrible life is on a vent. When I didn't bite and seriously consider what he explained because people have full lives on ventilators, he went behind my back and started on Lisa. He painted an extreme scenario saying how miserable life is predicting within six months I would be in a nursing home because she won't be able to handle my care. Dante's Inferno sounds pleasant in comparison.

During the final moments of breathing on my own, filled with stress and uncertainty, I received a dose of anger from his speculation and "opinion" on living. He couldn't comprehend that Lisa was already handling all the care needs he was warning about. An unrecognized blessing, over the last couple of years, my care slowly transitioned from what I could do to what Lisa needed to manage. She didn't have all my care needs thrust upon her in one overwhelming instant like someone with a spinal cord injury or stroke.

The absurdity of the doctor's opinion became apparent when both Lisa and my sister later said they saw him looking up what ALS was on the computer. We laugh about it in years to come because it's ridiculous to give such definitive advice based on a glance at a textbook definition. Had I not studied and became an advocate for myself, I would have died based on flawed information.

Tonight, I say goodbye to the family not only because of the possibility of my death but also, I may not speak after today. It depends on the trache type used and ALS factors with aspiration being the primary concern. I am not concerned about the surgery killing me but more worried about an infection taking advantage of my weakened state. I lost forty pounds from barely eating anything for months caused by breathing issues because I didn't have enough energy chewing and swallowing. It complicated my tongue and throat muscle weakness caused by ALS. Lou Gehrig's Disease viciously attacks everything. The ALS diet beats any other by a mile!

I have heartfelt conversations with my brother and sister, including what I want from them for Kelsey if I'm not around. However, the evening spent with Kelsey and Lisa is the most rewarding and challenging part of my goodbyes. The toll on Lisa is evident despite her efforts to hide it from me. She shows fantastic strength and love amid the devastating storm wreaking havoc on our lives. She's my rock.

Kelsey playing on my hospital bed brings me incredible joy seeing her precious little face. I also understand from her subdued expression that the room and the seriousness of the situation are impacting her no matter how much we fake happiness.

She's my little buddy. We play games, watch her shows, and I frequently become her makeup doll. Her big smile, sparkling eyes and hearing her call me Daddy are gifts from God. They're all the reasons I need to keep fighting.

It's also why I try holding my emotions in check, which takes all the strength I can muster. If my time on earth is ending, I want her to see me smiling and beaming love for her.

December 18 – The Midnight of Loneliness

After the emotional evening of final goodbyes, I'm exhausted to my core. Sleep should be easily achieved before the intubation procedure in the morning. They're doing it, so I breathe normally for a day or two before the tracheostomy surgery to strengthen me. They told me I would have no memory of the next three or four days. I find out later that had I waited until I was in respiratory failure and needed emergency intubation, I would have died. The unique physiology of my throat impacted by ALS caused a fifteen-minute procedure to take over two hours. My guardian angel looked out for me during this process.

That night when I'm alone, the fears and doubts about what I chose consume and overwhelm me. I stare at the clock as the second hand markedly slows when it strikes midnight. My mind races through worst-case scenarios. I panic at the life I committed to living. Maybe I should give up and die tonight. Will Lisa and Kelsey be better off without me since my family committed to helping in my stead, including financially?

I have visits from spirits of people who died recently in the hospital while still being aware of the living activity going on around me. The strange thing is I float above myself. The nurses appear to move as if they are running at fast forward speed. It's like the classic movie, The Time Machine. In whatever world I stumbled into, time is irrelevant, revealing that too much importance is placed on it instead of experiencing the remarkable, fascinating life around us.

During this, I realize a fellow is sitting in the room watching me and reassuring me I was never alone. He finally comes over, putting His hand on mine. I instantly recognize Jesus. He encourages me I a/m doing the right thing because He has plans for me. I was never and would never be alone. With that knowledge comforting me, I drift asleep.

An ICU Christmas

On December 17th, I was on the edge of death, but the next day of my memory, I experience the most fantastic rejuvenation of life. Not just from my breathing restoration but also the renewal of my spirit knowing that despite my broken body that my life has a higher purpose. It's Christmas when my family gathers in the ICU waiting room; I realize besides my unknown higher purpose, I also will have a fulfilling life, full of happiness. It's more than I ever imagined possible.

I lost my life, but persevering through the darkest, trying times when I wanted to give up, I found a new life. It's better than I dreamed or hoped for with a significant meaning beyond myself. Maybe waiting rooms aren't that bad after all. Everyone struggles for reasons big or small. Please find comfort in this; you're NEVER alone. You can change your life's direction. You are ALWAYS loved.

It matters not how strait the gate,
How charged with punishments the scroll,
I am the master of my fate:
I am the captain of my soul.

William Ernest Henley from Invictus, the final stanza

MY PRISON

My body became my prison
Powerless, helpless, pathetic, and weak

My body abandoned me
Unable to give a hug

My body let me down
Once young, full of life

My body gave up
The spirit never will

My body weakened
Mind grew stronger

My body turned soft and weak
Used to play football, hike, speak

My body became a scrap heap
I became greater than my body

My body is broken
The soul won't follow

My body crumbled
Making me humble

My body has become a prison
Yet God's love sets me free

SECTION 2

A LIFE WORTH LIVING IS A LIFE WELL LIVED

The Spirit God gave us does not make us timid,
but gives us power, love and self-discipline.

2 Timothy 1:7 (NIV)

Section one built a new life out of the ashes of the life ALS destroyed. It followed a chronological order from chapter to chapter. Section two follows a thematic approach. The story of my struggles and triumphs continues for three chapters.

After venting, ALS did its worst damage. Some people who vent, their relentless progression continues. They sometimes progress where they cannot move anything, including their eyes putting them in a locked-in state. It's a blessing for the twenty-plus years on a ventilator my progression stopped. The following description of my physical condition gives a glimpse into my day-to-day life. It provides a context for the remaining chapters.

My arms and legs lack any functional movement. My hands and feet slightly move. I maintain control of my head movement when sitting in my recliner critical for me to use a HeadMouse to operate my computer. A HeadMouse by Origin is a tracking system using lasers bouncing off a reflective dot on my glasses. It's more efficient and faster than the eye tracking system used by many in my condition. Technology gives back the independence I lost.

My head in other situations is like a rag doll where I have no control over it. My immediate family is the only people who understand my slurred speech. They serve as translators for anyone else. The most crucial ability I maintain is the ability to eat and drink many things. Most people with ALS must use a feeding tube within a few years of their diagnosis. The final insult ALS produced is my impaired swallowing causes drooling. It's an area where I'm more fortunate than most with Lou Gehrig's Disease. My worst day drooling is a regular day for many with ALS.

All these issues create complete dependency. Lisa does everything for me. It's aggravating not doing anything for myself, but I've learned to ignore the frustration otherwise it crushes me. I'm forced daily to learn patience beyond what I ever thought was possible. Embarrassment no longer exists in my world. It's eliminated maintaining my sanity.

When I'm away from home and family who understand me, life becomes harder and even dangerous when in a hospital. Imagine being put in a country where no one recognizes your language while knowing everything they say. Further, their customs differ from your norms for comfort, which is the situation faced when admitted to a hospital. Assumptions made about my condition cause me discomfort. Sometimes it becomes severe pain because I cannot communicate with the person caring for me. I see things done that threaten my health. I want to scream stop, but my inability to speak silences my protests.

Ordinary situations create grueling trials for people with ALS. An itch or worse a bug buzzing around an ear is agonizing. All you can do is pray it goes away. It tests your limits of sanity since you cannot seek relief provided by scratching. I discovered when you don't scratch an itch; it becomes worse. It screams to do something reminding me I can't do the simplest task.

Another issue that's upsetting is the inability to take part in conversations with multiple people involved. It silences me at family gatherings. Because of my ventilator, electricity is as vital to my life as food and water. For power outages, there are twelve hours of battery power. Ice storms aren't pleasant when they're looming in the weather forecast.

The issues aren't something I dwell on each day. They're complications for my new way of living. I trust God watches me and keeps me safe. He is always with me.

5

MOUNTAINS TO MOVE, STORMS TO WEATHER

Jesus said, "If you have faith as small as a mustard seed, you can say to this mountain, 'Move from here to there,' and it will move. Nothing will be impossible for you."

Matthew 17:20 (NIV)

In your life, sometimes the road seems wide and flat with no unexpected curves. The storms encountered in this section of your journey are gentle spring showers or softly falling snow. Both slow you down but bring with them the beauty that enhances your senses, creating joy and passion which poets pen odes and musicians compose ballads. Life is perfect.

However, if your entire story remains calm, you're not growing as a person. You are not stretching yourself beyond what's easy to broaden your horizons. Your life becomes dull and mundane. You stagnate and don't enjoy the vast splendor around you, causing you to wither and die. Some mountains in our way we exuberantly engage while others block our progress. Often when we have the test of mountains in our path, ferocious storms form. When we steer around them, they turn toward us, making our rough trip appear hopeless.

Starting a New Life

By going on a ventilator, I took a road most don't choose with ALS. The unknown territory makes the difficulties faced more daunting. We hope to create as ordinary a life as we can together. It's counter to the medical advice we received since the belief is nursing home care or 24/7 nursing assistance are necessary at home. When I came home, our dining area had turned into a hospital room. They expected I would stay in bed. It's not how I wished to spend my life.

The hospital bed provided is one step above a medieval torture device which isn't wide enough and too small for someone six feet, two inches tall. One night lost in the misery of our former dining room, it motivates the discovery of better ways to live. The next night I sleep in our regular king-sized bed with Lisa. After a night of blissful slumber and moving to my big La-Z-Boy, I never go back to a hospital bed.

With major hurdles to normal life removed, we realize everything they advised us needs to be questioned then either streamlined or eliminated. My healing from surgery requires immense patience. It's a slow process. The focus centers on avoiding any infections limiting our ability to try other ideas for my care. It takes six months for me to heal fully. It's like body piercings on a grander scale.

We spent the rest of the year tweaking and reducing my care needs. Restructuring procedures where they take less than five minutes instead of fifteen to thirty minutes using recommended practices, make our lives easier. We pared down the supplies where we have a home, not a hospital ward. Attention shifted to our family life, not my care and disability. We're happier with each step toward a normal world.

Through the trials and adjustments living on a ventilator, I learn the valuable lesson. Use my gut as my compass. Even when I'm wrong about something, I'm right about the overall goal. It's not uneducated impulses because we seek both medical advice and experiences of others before proceeding with any changes. I wish I discovered this before now.

Missing opportunities for happiness by valuing other people's opinions over my own frustrates me because it wasted time. I can live with being wrong on my judgment but not based on someone's view of what I should or should not do.

Into the Unknown

Our lives settled down after adjusting to a vent. There were the occasional health issues even emergencies like when the vent tube detached (called a pop off) for over thirty minutes. The alarm didn't wake Lisa. My breathing was an epic battle, but with God's aid, I persevered. Each instance reminds me what a precarious position my condition remains in now. Each case offers chances to find better and more reliable solutions for my care without compromising our goal, normalcy. I'm blessed my problems are few compared to most with Lou Gehrig's Disease. Because of this, I press the limits of my assumed boundaries.

Lisa agrees to babysit, Ryan, Greg's youngest, in March. He's a newborn. She still watches his five-year-old daughter, Tara, who is like a sister to Kelsey. With Tara also having three older brothers, Kelsey recognizes that she's without siblings. She requests a little brother or sister. At first, we don't give it any consideration since it's unheard of for someone with ALS on a vent having additional kids.

Over the summer, the time with Ryan makes us ponder the prospect. Why not have another child becomes the question. We defied conventional wisdom on almost every point for having ALS, especially on a ventilator but adding to our family is uncharted water. I might dream about it, but Lisa must lead on this decision. She's taking on added burdens for our family.

We eliminate most scenarios after the thoughtful debate, narrowing our choice between the benefits of Kelsey having special bonds with a sibling or not risking the unknown. We're debating back and forth between each scenario when an incomprehensible tragedy strikes, 9/11.

The world stops as horrific scenes unfold before our eyes. Lisa's sister, Sandi, lives in New York City. It takes all day before we learn she's safe. Her firsthand story of walking across the bridge from work, the smells, the fears, the utter destruction and loss suffered brings home what we see on television. My sister, Laura, is now a lawyer in DC and conveys similar feelings and events. The shared sense of grief and resolve to overcome the unthinkable disaster changes and briefly unites our nation.

It's a seminal moment because it reminds us how disasters strike anyone in an instant and show how the family is who we lean on with God's love. The result, we're having another child! With that settled, Lisa and I now venture into the unknown arena of expanding our family.

When Lisa becomes pregnant, I shock my family with fantastic news. My brother's reaction sums up their shock, "How?" Everyone assumed ALS rendered me impotent! The only reply I can muster from laughing so hard is "The usual way!" We plan for our new addition, including for my care, when Lisa is having our baby. We soon learn we are having another daughter, Emily. In February, Lisa finds a house across from Kelsey's elementary school she loves. We move to our new home in March. My wife amazes me with her strength caring for Kelsey and me, babysitting our niece and nephew, and moving all while being very pregnant.

In July, everything is going smooth when Lisa has problems with gestational diabetes. It's uncertain planning for an early August due date. Between my family and the St. Louis Chapter of the ALS Association paying for my respite nurse, Sue, to cover my care, we're confident in our plan. However, as Lisa's diabetes worsens, her condition becomes concerning. I can bear whatever my illness throws at me and accept whatever limitations people place on me.

God, please don't ask me to take a world where Lisa's harmed or not here. She's the cog in our small, growing family. When diabetes gets worse on her next appointment, the doctor wants to induce. Lisa convinces him to delay it until the following day so we can start our plan. I have worried little with all I've been through Lord because I trust in You, I pray You will protect Lisa and our baby, Emily. On July 20, our family grows without incident. Thank you, God!

Believing we survived potential devastation, we revel in the joy of our new family. Little do we know a significant storm is gathering. After Thanksgiving, we learn that Lisa's dad is sick with a kidney infection. He is only fifty-four, so it doesn't seem critical. After a few days, her mom tells Lisa they rushed him to the hospital. Something in my gut tells me she needs to go to Springfield. It's over two hours from us, so Lisa takes Emily with her for what we believe is an overnight trip.

When they get there, she finds out it's more severe because of a heart issue her father put off addressing. It causes a situation where the doctors cannot solve either problem without complicating the other. Lisa visits her dad for several hours, where he holds Emily while they talk. She leaves Cox Hospital with her mom to the attached hotel while the doctors place a stint. They arrive in the room when they receive an urgent call to rush back because Butch, Lisa's dad, had a massive heart attack. He dies before they get back.

It's a week until I see Lisa and Emily again. It's bad enough I cannot support her mourning her loss but worse, I cannot hold her to comfort her when she's home. I'm more disabled in these moments than ever before. It's the lowest point of my journey with ALS.

Surprise!

We settled into a pleasant routine for our family of four, which is remarkable given my health condition. My being the sole boy in a family of girls presents an eye-opening experience since I grew up with Dad and Greg. I find satisfaction in helping others with ALS. It's strange becoming an elder within the ALS community because of my longevity even though I'm still younger than most being diagnosed. Writing blogs and hosting chat boards giving advice and support are most gratifying. I wrote articles published for the MDA magazine, Quest.

I redeveloped a passion for writing when I started working with a family friend, Robert Vaughan, a successful author, for a Boy Scout merit badge. It's one of those childhood dreams pushed aside during the relentless march to adulthood. The reboot of my life permits entertaining hopes of being a writer again. I built a satisfying and fulfilling life for someone supposed to perish alone seven years ago. I don't allow myself to consider a future beyond a year. My focus centers on the miracle of today. No mountain appears impossible to conquer because, with the power God gave me, I chip away until nothing's left in my path.

As the summer days wane and we adjust to a new school year for Kelsey, a seismic shift shakes our lives. Lisa's pregnant! The pregnancy brings both incredible joy and grave concern. Besides the immediate aspect of Lisa's health during her last pregnancy, there is a broader picture that a new child stretches our resources. It means finding a bigger house.

The already small house became stuffed when we invited Lisa's mother, Suzie, and her two yappy dogs to move in with us. She can't regain her footing after Butch's unfortunate death two years ago. Alone and mired in a state of depression put her life in a downward spiral. She's not capable of pulling herself out. We invited her to live with us because, while we have little, we possess a wealth of love with our two daughters. We believe that's the best cure for her. Isn't family about supporting each other?

Emily becomes my new computer buddy like Kelsey was at her age. She possesses a unique spunk. Emily adores her older sister. When we tell Kelsey and Emily, we're expecting a little brother or sister, they're thrilled. Everything moves along smoothly until around Thanksgiving when Lisa gets diabetes again. It started sooner than with Emily, which we expected, but this soon causes unease. We adjust our daily routine, reducing Lisa's physical stress. The most notable difference, she's unable to lift me into a manual wheelchair for transfers to and from the bed. I realize the time before Lisa can lift me again; I will lose the strength in my legs to bear any weight. I wasn't standing much since Lisa deadlifts my now one-hundred-and-ninety-pound body. The few seconds, I was upright each day, provided my last trace of physical normality. Our dance happened twice a day for eight years. While it's remarkable it lasted this long, losing it is a painful reminder of my severe disability.

By late January, we adapt to changes in our daily routine. It now includes a Hoyer lift for moves between the bed and my recliner. It reminds me of lifts you see mechanics use putting engines in cars. I'm the motor in our scenario. The Hoyer becomes a piece of gymnastics equipment for Emily. She spins on it like a circus acrobat, making herself stumble like a drunken sailor when she's done. It highlights each day producing a good belly laugh for anyone who sees it.

I'm coughing more, which is not surprising during the winter months, but it typically ebbs and flows from day to day. This cough persists and worsens. More troubling, it becomes painful and turns into a brown color. My pulmonologist, who makes regular home visits, is worried enough to come here in the afternoon after Lisa called this morning. After a quick examination, he points out that my nail beds are blue and explains it's a serious if not life-threatening lung infection. He calls for an ambulance and arranges for my admission into the ICU. It's the first time since going on the vent I feel close to death.

Fortunately, with Lisa's mom living with us, she watches for Kelsey and Emily. I am still worried that my being sick puts too much stress on Lisa at this stage in her pregnancy. Over the next few days, it's touch and go as the doctors locate the correct drugs to wipe out the various bacteria causing the problem. I have moments where fear overwhelms me breaking me down in those brief periods of doubt.

Overall, I don't fear death. I recognize God has plans for me, and besides, each day I hang on the precipice of death living on a ventilator. Over time, I became calloused toward the prospect of dying; otherwise, it would consume my every thought, my life. After a week, I feel well. I want out, but the IV antibiotic therapy has another week before it's completed. I can finish them at home, but we learned over the eight years that the medical community is cautious with someone on a vent. It takes several days for my release.

After being home a few days, Suzie, my mother-in-law, declares she would rather die than live like me. At first, I am taken aback by her rude declaration. It's not the first time someone said something, and it won't be the last, but other statements weren't blunt. After pondering what she said, I realize it's more about her life than it is about mine.

As much as we hoped living with us provided her with joy and a renewed sense of purpose, it hasn't. I better understand the phrase you can lead a horse to water, but you can't make it drink. Suzie cannot understand the happy and fulfilling life I have because she's lost in the darkness of bitterness and resentment over the life she lost. The veil of darkness controls every emotion and action in her life. A new life is hers for the taking if she would remove the sad mask. She doesn't fathom I would never trade places with her to live the life she's living.

April is a relief to reach since Jordan's due date is the twenty-second. A third daughter means I'm becoming a small island in a sea of females in this Lester family. We knew the due date was not a reality since Lisa's gestational diabetes became an issue. We planned for an early delivery, including my being admitted to the hospital for the days around the birth. It's easier on everyone involved, including me. On the morning of April sixth, Lisa's doctor appointment reveals diabetes turned serious. Even worse, she developed high blood pressure. The doctor preferred to admit her, but she's determined to come home and set in motion things herself.

That afternoon, I leave by ambulance to the ICU after convincing Lisa I can handle everything from this point. My family took her in before I left. The next hours are a dreamlike experience for the staff and me at St. John's Hospital. I don't imagine they encounter many festive events beyond recoveries from severe injury and illness. I came in with a big smile on my face and shared the joyous anticipation with the entire unit.

It's a huge relief when the first reports come in, they've controlled Lisa's blood pressure and diabetes. They induced her starting the countdown to another daughter. It's funny having my medical staff interpret each report on how things are progressing. It's like watching football with John Madden.

The excitement builds as midnight approaches. An aide tells me her birth could happen at any moment. When my nurse comes into my room with a huge grin, I know I am a new dad. Later, I hear awes as a maternity nurse brings Jordan to meet me for the first time. For someone expected to die alone, my cup runs over. God is great!

Darkest Before the Dawn

This past spring, I researched options for pursuing a master's degree through an online program. It's a hole from my previous life that I could not fill or forget and move on to new endeavors. Maybe because it's the goal I was chasing when ALS totaled my life or because my parents instilled it in me for my educational pursuits. The unfulfilled promise gnawed at me for thirteen years. Lou Gehrig's Disease took away an essential part of my sense of self. Online technology and my survival made it a reality. I didn't like the for-profit schools, but after searching, I discovered the University of Michigan-Dearborn. UMD is a public, highly rated program.

While my undergraduate grades and GMAT test score exceed their average admission standards, I learned after ten years, GMAT discards all test scores. I don't prefer to retake the test since that presents physical challenges, but undeterred, I write the dean of UMD's business college explaining my dilemma. ALS taught me if you approach life with a nothing to lose attitude, extraordinary things occur. I still fail and risk rejection but realize those are minor in the bigger scheme of life. My biggest regrets from my life before ALS aren't the losses suffered, but when I didn't stretch my boundaries trying something.

The response received from the Dean supports my application. He encourages me to apply. This is the first time since having ALS that anyone supports doing something outside my disabled world. When I receive the admission letter to be a full-time graduate student at UMD, I am over the moon with delight. The Dean taking a chance on me, produces an opportunity to expand my limits. Sometimes someone needs to provide you a chance, but it's what you do with the moment that defines how you live. It's a terrific yet daunting prospect of becoming a student again after seventeen years.

Trying to fund my studies, I contact Missouri Vocational Rehabilitation (Voc-Rehab) whose purpose is helping disabled people get jobs. It includes assisting with academic pursuits. When the caseworker visits my home, I'm excited to hear how much help I might qualify for from the program. The meeting doesn't go as hoped. After I explain my plan and goals with Lisa translating so the caseworker understands, she declares my idea to get a graduate degree is absurd. She tells us that my aim to gain full employment getting off government benefits is too ambitious. She urges me to work enough to maximize what I can earn and still receive on Social Security, about $750 per month. Game the system is her suggestion.

My head nearly explodes. She may be correct about my objectives, but it's improper for her to discourage getting off governmental aid. It's offensive for someone who has no clue about my capabilities to tell me anything is unattainable. I have grown sick and tired of being told what I cannot do because of ALS since I proved to myself nothing's impossible if you keep faith in yourself and God. Little does my caseworker know she lit a fire in me to prove her prediction wrong.

It's a week before my classes start. My excitement soars with a little doubt mixed in centered on my nervousness about my statistics class. Nineteen years have passed since my last college math class, so I needed to brush up my math skills. The other uncertainty involves the process surrounding being a disabled student, which includes getting required textbooks converted to an electronic form. This means buying a textbook which they cut apart for scanning.

UMD's disability office tops my expectations by helping with issues and working with my professors. Still, venturing into the unknown is frightening. It's the constant state of my life since being diagnosed, so I should be used to it. Absorbed in a statistic help book, I see Lisa coming toward me with a letter in hand. She's pale with tears forming in her eyes.

My long-term disability company, Unum, who bought my policy last year, claims my plan overpaid me since Kelsey's birth in 1995. They now say twelve years later that I must repay the total overpayment amount of $65,000 or they withhold my new reduced monthly benefit until I refund the shortfall. It means even if I live until sixty-five, I won't receive income from them. I had a bad feeling since seeing a 60 Minutes segment about Unum. We made no mistakes reporting anything. This was my old insurance company, Paul Revere's, error. They destroy my family's life because of it.

When you live on Social Security and long-term disability, you're careful planning, but you believe it's secure income. Children and buying a house depend on that security. We purchased our first home last year. Unum assured our income for the mortgage company. The troubling part is the Social Security benefit for the care of children caused the overpayment, and the reduction is a legal loophole, that's part of my policy. I realize it's not a real benefit for children, but a backdoor government handout for insurance companies.

The stress overwhelms Lisa and me. It's not like Lisa can get a regular job outside the house to make up the difference because of my care needs. Some suggest Lisa get a job without understanding the effects on our family. It causes serious financial repercussions because we're unable to pay debt since we lost thirty percent of our income. It's a problematic beginning for my academic pursuits creating moments of doubt, causing me to question if continuing under the specter of gathering storms is the correct path. I separate the student pressures from the issues confronting my family. I put my head down and soldier on. The situation lessens the thrill of my new quest.

The Final Nail

I gain my footing after toiling a month adjusting to the work involved with a full load of graduate classes. I become more determined to excel after people make ignorant negative comments that online education is inferior and less demanding. This isn't the case since classmates who already possess graduate degrees from renowned schools say how rigorous our classes are. Many are executives at Ford and Google or officers in the military. I trust their opinions. In my forties, I'm the old man amongst students ten to twenty years younger than me. It's not lost on me being the old man outliving the ALS prognosis.

Approaching important papers due by Thanksgiving with finals following the break, Lisa's work-from-home job laid her off. The paycheck is $600 per month. In our precarious financial position, the loss is crushing. We're victims of the great recession. For my family, we lost half our income in a matter of months just before Christmas.

It's the tipping point forcing us out of the home we worked hard buying.

There is no worse feeling than knowing your family is on the brink of homelessness and you can't do anything to avoid it. This shakes my strong faith in God. It's one thing to go down an unknown, difficult path when you're alone; it's unbearable when you're taking the road with your wife and daughters.

A New Frontier

As expected, we're forced to leave our home. We suffer humiliation from being put in this position. We're moving away from the city that's been home our entire marriage. The area, known as West County in St. Louis, is no longer an option given our financial condition since it's expensive. We scraped by before losing income. The impending change is tough for Kelsey, who is in the seventh grade because she's losing her friends and school at an age when it's her entire world.

Once West County was not a choice, we agreed on Lebanon, Missouri, Lisa's hometown. Her mom, grandmother, and cousins live there plus she has friends living there. Since I am a small-town boy, there's peace raising our daughters in the same environment. Still, the severity of my condition in a small medical community and not having my family, who sometimes helped, puts us in unfamiliar territory. It's not ideal with Lou Gehrig's Disease. Our rush into this situation because of financial problems causes a severe strain on our family, especially Lisa.

One of the worst parts of having ALS is being an observer and a burden in moving situations because I'm physically useless. More upsetting, the move disrupts my daily routine, which causes health distress making my care problematic. Nothing saddens me more than the trouble I create for Lisa in these moments. Seeing my wife and children in dire straits, I want to do anything and everything for them. All I can do is minimize my care needs.

After Lisa falls asleep, I often break down because of our crisis. I feel guilty and ask God for help since I don't know how much more my family or I can bear.

A Blessing in Disguise

Sometimes the worst situations lead to unexpected, positive outcomes. When you face hopeless odds amid a devastating storm, you don't see the hope for better days on the horizon. You trudge forward step-by-step, trusting God leads you to the right path. This is the essence of faith.

Moving to Lebanon, we were blind to what it meant for our family and my unique care needs, so finding a nice house was more difficult than we thought. Most house rentals in any area within our budget involve stairs to the bedroom or some split-level living area. My disability removes those options restricting our choices. It added stress since we have a firm deadline to move from the home that we lost to foreclosure. Limited options and renting in the winter are not a good mix.

We find a two-year-old house, within our budget, and fitting our needs available on March 1. It's the nicest home we have ever had. It's a miracle considering months ago we were worried about being homeless or being forced into undesirable living conditions. God provides!

The most dreaded part of our move is how our kids will adjust. Will kids in Lebanon accept them? Any parent moving to a new area with kids in school confronts this truth. When you include my physical disability into the mix, it adds another level of concern. I fear my presence may cause my daughter's friends to spurn them when they visit our home. It hasn't happened to this point.

Our daughters adjust quickly and thrive in Lebanon. Our church, The First United Methodist Church of Lebanon, becomes a foundation for the girls and a vital support system for our family. Kelsey blossoms into an amazing young woman and graduates valedictorian after being the head cheerleader her senior year.

I'm delighted my care hasn't become more burdensome. It's difficult imagining but realizing we don't have backup permitted us to push the boundaries of my care needs. It allows Lisa more freedom than before. Despite the chaos during the first year at UMD, God gave me the strength and inner peace to achieve all A grades. After four years, I accomplish a higher GPA than in high school or as an undergraduate. I graduated with Distinction with two master's degrees, an M.B.A., and an MS in Finance 2011.

I attended my graduation ceremony in Dearborn, Michigan, after a successful campaign to get me there. Friends and family donated to help cover the cost for my family and me even holding a fundraising event called Lester Launch in my hometown of Sikeston. The outpouring of support I received from my friends in Sikeston was overwhelming. The campaign even received national media attention after a story in the Springfield News-Leader ran in USA Today.

A nightmare turned into a dream ended up better than my wildest fantasy. I had serious doubts along the way, not just about my family's well-being, but also if I would live through it. Now, I'm going on twenty years with ALS feeling stronger than ever. I never lost faith. God was leading us down the better path though occasionally I couldn't see the way through, and sometimes storms seemed never-ending. God knew He was leading us to greener pastures. We were blessed by following His lead!

The Sign

When life becomes calm and the road too smooth, I get wary of what's coming since these periods are short-lived since my journey with ALS began. We became more adept at handling and expecting disorder in our lives. When the calm breaks with another impending storm, we're not surprised.

This storm comes in the form of a for sale sign being placed in our yard in late August. The odds are whoever buys our house will live here or will raise our rent. Either scenario forces us to move. After studying what's vacant for renting, we realize the timing couldn't be worse with few houses available and nothing that meets our minimum requirement of no stairs. Buying isn't an option since we're still under the financial clouds that forced us to move here.

It's a long fall and winter praying there isn't a buyer. Winter is the worst-case scenario for our family because it has the fewest rentals, and cold weather exposure is terrible for someone on a ventilator. The dryness causes lung irritation, which triggers infections.

Not having muscle and fat, something I wouldn't think was a problem before ALS, makes me prone to chills producing uncontrollable shaking. It gets so severe that my jaw will violently clench catching my tongue. Some with ALS bite parts of their tongue off. Fortunately, my jaw clenches only caused minor bleeding so far. I pray for things to hold off until spring when it's warmer and rental houses come available.

Ice Storm Cometh

All's quiet on the house front. No one has looked at the house since October. Winter brings potential terror for someone on a ventilator, an ice storm. Everyone hates them. When your life depends on electricity for heat and to breathe, it's a real storm that strikes fear to your core. The mix of losing power, my cold sensitivity, and the risk that help can't get to us for days create my perfect storm.

Tonight, KY3 weatherman, Ron Hearst, predicts a significant ice event occurring with the bullseye of an inch or more centered on Lebanon. I go over the options in my mind making tonight a sleepless night.

Should we stay with family in St. Louis? What if the storm shifts and we're stuck there? Should I go to the hospital before the storm hits? These, along with a dozen other scenarios, race through my mind. Ultimately, one thought prevails. What will it do to my family if I die being stuck in an ice storm? I am unconcerned about my death on a personal level because I prepared for it since 1993. It's the guilt my family could carry seeing me die from a stupid decision where they cannot save me.

The next day when the forecast remains unchanged, I seek prayers from friends on Facebook, asking for the storm us shift and dissipate. It isn't something I enjoy asking of people. I believe in the power of prayer. I feel if asking someone to give their spirit in prayer for my benefit, the request needs to be urgent and meaningful. Here, it's hard asking since the prayers might mean shifting the trouble to someone else.

Once I ask, the predicted ice storm moves south and becomes weaker, and when the storm hits, it barely turns off any electricity. The ice storm diminishing wasn't from prayer; some may say. I know prayers were the reason the storm passed. Does praying always mean you get whatever you request? No, ALS taught me that prayers are appeals to God, not magic wishes. He might not answer them how you want, but God answers your prayers.

The House Next Door

Spring arrives! We survived winter without moving. They pulled our house off the market after the ice storm threat. However, we learn it's a matter of time before our home goes back up for sale. We search for rental houses understanding later this month, and June are prime opportunities for locating a new place.

A heaven-sent answer comes when a for rent sign appears in the house's yard next door! Built after we moved here, it includes four bedrooms instead of three like we have now. The owners, Jim and Penny, are our neighbors. They're caring people who regularly help.

Whatever obstacle or storm life lies in our path, God's grace allows us to overcome it. No matter how voracious the storm or devastating it seems, placing faith in God is essential. Continuing to push forward on the map He placed in my heart guided me to better, happier places isn't easy when things look bleak. I had severe doubts and moments I wanted to quit during my journey with Lou Gehrig's Disease. If I give up, God patiently waits by my side, picks me up, dusts me off, and sends me on my way as any good parent does.

God doesn't want us ashamed of these momentary failures because we are human, not perfect. God cheers us on to better days ahead. I learned it's unnecessary to beat yourself up for perceived shortcomings. God considers you perfect the way you are, so why are you questioning yourself?

"We are experiencing all kinds of trouble, but we aren't crushed. We are confused, but we aren't depressed. We are harassed, but we aren't abandoned. We are knocked down, but we aren't knocked out ...
All these things are for your benefit. As grace increases to benefit more and more people, it will cause gratitude to increase,
which results in God's glory."

2 Corinthians 4:8-9,15

6

ENDURANCE OF FAITH

We even take pride in our problems, because we know that trouble produces endurance, endurance produces character, and character produces hope. This hope doesn't put us to shame, because the love of God has been poured out in our hearts through the Holy Spirit, who has been given to us.

Romans 5:3-5

One of the toughest parts of life is enduring conditions you cannot control. Everyone suffers the experience of surviving situations, people, and even themselves at points in their lives. It falls on the range from tolerating boredom to existing in extreme mental, physical, emotional or spiritual pain. Sometimes, a simultaneous assault occurs on all four aspects of your life, causing extreme stress and discomfort. The battering drains your spirit, sucking you down into hopeless misery. The torment on your life unleashes potential damage on people around you where they become innocent bystander victims.

Your reaction marks a crossroad for your life that forever changes it and others. What will you do? Do you turn toward or away from God? The decisions reflect the person you are and direct who you become. It overshadows the problems that brought you to this juncture. The moments of agony shape, refine, and cause a possible complete redesign of your life. When you're going through it, you either find strength for bearing the burden, or it breaks you.

Your resilience depends on the foundation you built before confronting the uncontrollable events. Often, we celebrate the strength of those who seem unbreakable under pressure holding them up as heroes. People who break get marginalized and forgotten. Their failure stamps them with the mark of weakness and shame. This shouldn't happen because God wants us to celebrate and uplift both with equal love and understanding. You never know when it's your time for testing.

When a river forms scenery over the ages developing splendor by peeling back the outer layers of land, revealing what's below explains endurance. The majesty of the Grand Canyon displays God's patience creating beauty through flaws. Powerful forces transform us forever.

The New Madrid Earthquakes of 1811-12 show how influential the changes are. They rang bells in Boston. Native tribes read the strong shakings as signs making them join a war against the European settlers. The quakes altered the Mississippi River. They created waterfalls within the river. It flowed backward making Reelfoot Lake in Tennessee.

When diagnosed with a disease such as ALS, it permanently changes you becoming your personal Great New Madrid Earthquake. No matter how much you may try to resist, your life journey certainly flows in another direction. It's your choice to become stubborn, defying the inevitable changes wasting time and assuring your destruction or hold on and see where God leads you.

Does this mean don't fight? No, it means you reserve your strength for the battles you can win. With ALS, I couldn't alter the toll it took on my body or the ruin of my former life, so resisting those fronts is a fool's errand. Fighting for the new life where God led me and taking my destiny away from Lou Gehrig's Disease was the war I fought and won with His help. I endure the ravages of ALS daily, but now it's on my terms.

Endurance is more challenging when you're dependent. You're a prisoner of your body, making you helpless. The condition itself creates unimaginable epic scenarios. When you're disabled, a simple itch becomes trouble. You don't realize what before was a reflex reaction becomes a painful process to get help. Given Lou Gehrig's Disease's speech impact, it quickly gives into a tiresome search for relief frustrating you and the poor soul chosen for aid.

I discovered early with ALS that when you're unable to scratch yourself; the body doesn't tolerate being ignored. It turns up the intensity of a common itch to a poison ivy level mandatory scratching in seconds. When I find myself in the unpleasant position of needing a good scratch, I remember my childhood Disney movie, The Jungle Book. Baloo the Bear expresses satisfaction in a good scratch. It wasn't until now I appreciate the pure brilliance of his musings! I learned when you're in situations where you have no control to find humor in it.

Abiding People

I want to be clear in the estimated forty-five days I have spent in St. John's, now Mercy, hospitals both in Creve Couer and Lebanon, Missouri, the following is not the typical quality of care I receive.

Hospital shift changes are small worries since I have been on a ventilator. My being a quadriplegic with a speech problem, I'm not effective in communicating even my basic needs. The most patient and understanding nurses and aides who give maximum effort comprehending what I say can easily misinterpret my requests. I learned the patience of Job speaking with anyone outside of my wife and three daughters. I appreciate everyone who tries understanding me, so I only get frustrated when someone does not attempt to comprehend me. Even worse is when a person assumes my inability to speak means I am mentally challenged, making it somehow acceptable to dismiss me.

When I was a teenager, I spent a summer volunteering at the Kenny Rogers Children's Center in Sikeston. It serves children with special needs and developmental delays. I have a much deeper appreciation for the challenges they face and now realize they wanted you to try. That's all I want. It's why I fear shift changes in hospitals.

You never know if essential information about how I communicate passes to the next group, meaning I could lose the ability to express what I need. It's when they tell about my limitations, and they give care needs, so it's a real-life version of the kid's game telephone that has serious consequences. The other issue is the person's disposition you're dealing with for the next twelve hours of your life. Are they thoughtful, stern, forgetful, sweet, stringent in their routine? I have experienced many combinations of people. The nurse and aide rarely have different caregiver personalities meaning your team for the shift don't offer relief in their differences. It's either the aide must follow the nurse's lead or the scheduling nurse pairs similar people. When you're utterly dependent on someone else, it's critical they have a good temperament. You hope you don't look like their ex who broke their heart!

When I see my new nurse seems experienced, it gives me a sense of relief because green ones in the ICU become overwhelmed by the demands of the unit. I notice the new nurse blowing off the outgoing nurse, it's a little concerning. Her attitude is dismissive, superior, blunt, and jerky. When her approach continues as she's instructed on my needs, mainly head position and communication, I want to scream, "Listen!" since it's critical for my safety and comfort. I'm only here for a procedure on my hip the next morning, so it's not like most visits being sick on top of my physical disability. Fortunately, I figure I won't have much interaction with her because I sleep most of her shift. I can take the discomfort coming from her ignorance. It's not as if I worry about being harmed by her.

The aide who feeds me dinner tries communicating with me on a fundamental level, so that eases some of my apprehension. I don't realize it will be the last time I see her the rest of the shift. When she finishes with my meal, she gets the nurse to reposition me. I have seen the nurse twice. She only made one thinly veiled attempt to understand me, but I could tell from the brevity and the blank stare she didn't care if she could.

It doesn't surprise me when during the repositioning process, they ignore me. Lisa gave explicit instructions that my head is like a rag doll's head flopping in whatever direction momentum takes it. They pay no attention to it as I'm flipped around giving me whiplash. When I express pain with each movement throwing my head where only the bones in my neck stop any further motion, they provide no care for my obvious distress.

I know people can't recognize my spoken words. However, there's no way they misunderstand my sounds of agony. I grasp the gravity of my predicament when the nurse leaves my head in an extreme position toward my right shoulder. Their only concern is they fulfilled the required movement from one side to the other.

The excruciating pain hits as the weight of my head stretches the tendons and ligaments to their breaking point. After a few minutes, other painful positions reveal themselves. My toes crush against the foot of the bed. My hip and shoulder scream in agony from the weight put on them. Even worse, my right pinky finger is squeezed against the bed rail causing excruciating pain.

For a moment, I chuckle to myself. The agonizing pinky brings back memories of my older brother's torture, making me cry out uncle. Little did we realize he was preparing me for this mess since I was stubborn about giving in to his demand.

The discomfort grows in intensity with each passing second. The clock appears broken like before my trache surgery when seconds became minutes or even hours. I'm ready to scream when the nurse returns to give me my nightly medicine. With head in an extreme position, I only moan. UNCLE!!!

Believing I am about to be rescued, I smile while getting the nurse's attention. She disrespects my pleas for help. I see another problem developing when she fills a cup with water for me to take the pills. I am sure my chart says I cannot drink water because it can choke me since the previous nurse came in with juice without asking. When the nurse comes rolling the hospital tray with the pills and a cup of water on it, she still doesn't see my distress.

My only choice is pursing my lips when she tries to force the first pill in my mouth. She starts kind telling me, loud and slow; this is medicine. I don't know where the misconceptions come from, but having speech issues many assume; you're hard of hearing and mentally impaired. After the initial attempt, she steps back slightly and asks me what the problem is. Finally, she's paying attention. It gives me a chance to communicate my dilemma. When I open my mouth to talk, the nurse attempts to force a pill in my mouth. I shut my yap. After she does it a second time popping a pill in my mouth, I promptly spit it out. I realize she's not asking me what's wrong instead she's asking why I'm a problem!

The question itself is a ploy getting me to open my mouth. How do I get across that I'm not being obstinate but have a legitimate issue when the other person refuses any attempt to communicate? While I get frustrated, the nurse gets angry. We go a few more rounds of questions to get me to open my mouth. When I don't open it that pisses her off more and once she comprehends I'm on to her game, she resorts to brute force. With each effort, she uses more pressure. She bloodies my lip and causing what I call an ALS clench. The nurse huffs out of the room. I can't tell what she mumbles as she leaves, but her body language tells me it's something like "I'll show him!" That's never good. What's the name of the evil nurse in that Jack Nicholson movie? Only eleven hours until the hospital's shift change.

An ALS clench is a powerful spasm in your jaw that's so uncontrollable some with ALS bite part of their tongue off if it catches in their teeth. Once that occurred, even if I wanted to open my mouth, it wasn't an option.

It's ten minutes before the nurse returns. I hope she took time to cool off. When I see her glaring at me as she prepares something on the counter, I see she hasn't cooled off because she looks angrier. I don't understand this person's issue with me because even if I was difficult, there is no excuse for her to become mad much less abusive.

As the nurse approaches me, she has an evil grin on her face and tells me I should have just taken the pills. She informs me with a hint of joy in her voice she's putting in a feeding tube. Ironically, she must move me off my side and straighten my head, which gives my voice back. I try explaining what was wrong, but with the stress, my speech is more slurred than usual. The nurse mocks my speech like elementary school bullies! What? No way that just happened. When I try speaking again, she starts with the same mocking only this time she gets in my face doing it. It causes anger to well up in me like a volcano about to erupt.

What sort of human thinks this behavior is okay? They're not someone with a shred of human decency or compassion. There's no excuse for horrific behavior. Getting some twisted pleasure from it speaks volumes about the person's evil character. This can't be happening. As she lays the feeding tube kit on my belly, the nurse tells me she won't be using any lubricant, making an already painful procedure more so. In another derisive gesture, she asks me for my consent. I say loud and clear, no!

She undeniably understands since her perverse laugh tells me no isn't an option. The nurse jams the tube into my left nostril. I immediately taste and feel the blood it's causing along with the throbbing pain I haven't experienced in youthful fist fights. I remember from the time I had the flu and having this procedure done; they instructed me to swallow. The tube goes down. Thank you, God, it's about over.

She sees relief come over my face upsetting her. The nurse grinning tells me it's wrong, so she violently yanks it out, causing me to gag. Despite my not wanting to give in to this psychotic individual who gets pleasure from my pain, I can't help myself when she taunts me with the same question. Do you give consent? My voice screams no along with some expletives. My eyes see as she jams the tube up the right nostril, I have given her twisted soul the feedback it desires.

She broke me. I want this torturous violation over. Satisfied, she leaves me in an equally painful position on my left side. I remember the movie, *One Flew Over the Cuckoo's Nest.* What is that sadistic nurse's name? Only ten and a half hours until shift change.

Livid at the physical and emotional abuse I endured for a little while time speeds up. Then the reality of my total disability and helplessness defending myself washes over me in a wave of self-pity and fear. It's something I logically knew, but I don't focus on my limitations in my daily life; instead, I discover the joy in what I can accomplish. I'm blessed God gave me the gift of viewing my life through the lens of possibilities, not the restrictions of my impossibilities.

Being slapped in the face with the reality of my physical vulnerability makes me weep at what I am now enduring. God, why do I or anyone become temporary slaves to abusers who gain more power than us in this life? My sadness slows the time somewhat. When the overwhelming discomfort of my body creeps back into my thoughts, time again screeches to a halt. Each second is a step closer to my escape and a reminder that much more is coming before I reach sweet relief.

The nurse returns, informing me I must urinate. How much longer will I be in this appalling woman's grip? It's difficult enough for me peeing in the hospital under normal circumstances. Now I have this merciless drill sergeant standing over me barking orders for me to go already every five seconds. I catch myself begging my bladder to just do it! It provides me with the briefest moment of levity, thinking this isn't what the commercial had in mind.

The nurse interrupts the reprieve when I grasp her real intention for pressuring me; she wants to put in a urinary catheter. We made it crystal clear I don't need or want one, so the gravity of this realization makes going on demand more difficult. After two minutes, the nurse declares that as she suspected I need a catheter because I can't inconvenience her. What?!? It's as much about her laziness as it is about her treating me like a piece of garbage.

It's easier to dismiss someone when you think they're somehow inferior or deserve their condition. It excuses treating people with inhumane behavior. I protest loud as she prepares for the procedure. I explicitly say no as many times as possible, hoping someone rescues me from the clutches of this heartless soul. Then her true colors come out, "Shut up, you fucking retard!" as she rapes my manhood forcefully shoving the catheter in me. I allow my mind to drift toward a place where I wasn't defenseless, only eight hours and forty-five minutes until the shift change.

The direct physical and mental assault end after the rape incident, but I remain on my side for over four and a half hours. Neglect becomes a painful reminder of my vulnerability. The little movement I have provides momentary relief, but it puts me in worse and more uncomfortable positions. I resist moving until things turn unbearable. I yell out for help whenever someone walks by room, but Nurse Ratched closes the sliding glass doors silencing me. Hey, that's the name of the nurse in the movie! I take small victories at this point.

I forgot Lisa was coming early before my hip procedure, so her arrival an hour before the shift change brings me unexpected elation. She delivers me from this hell I endured. When Lisa sees the feeding tube, the dried blood remaining below my nose, and the slight swelling looking like I was in a fight, my condition shocks her. Exhausted, I try holding my emotions in check despite the ordeal I experienced. I don't want to deal with Nurse Ratched spinning lies and don't want her removing the tube and catheter. It takes awhile conveying that my nurse is the problem.

Once Lisa understands some of what I've been through, she gets a supervisor to undo the handy work from the night. By the time another nurse does everything, the shift change occurs, so my attacker slinks away in the morning's fog. I get Lisa to file a formal complaint against the nurse, but I don't have the energy to relive the real horrors she put me through. Plus, they quickly prep for the procedure, and by the afternoon I'm released.

I write several emails detailing my experience, which they acknowledge but never act on the complaints. That adds insult to my injury since St. John's, now Mercy Hospital, ignored my violations at the hands of their nurse. As evidenced by my lack of ever pursuing legal action, I never wanted payment for the agony I suffered. I tried to prevent others from enduring abuse.

I have no profound answers to why I suffered physical and verbal abuse. Maybe the brief stay in the darkness of an abusive person was so I can give voice to those who bear far worse for much longer in loneliness and silence.

There are countless reasons individuals in powerful positions abuse the weak and vulnerable. Part of it is devaluing a person's worth and contribution to the world. It allows someone to dehumanize and mistreat another since they possess little or no value in their eyes. I experienced this phenomenon in more ways than extreme hospital abuse. There are the subtle dismissals of my opinion because I am disabled and on government help, so how can

I understand a "real world" problem. The devaluing attitude finds fertile ground believing disability implies I must be agreeable to whatever someone else wants. It leads some to try taking advantage with false friendship and help. I learned this lesson when a supposed good friend only came around to help for their financial gain.

The worst issue, being ignored and forgotten because I no longer live a so-called normal life. God doesn't want us acting this way. It's proven when Christ teaches that the least amongst us is the greatest in the next life. He also said how we treat the less fortunate our paths cross is how we have treated Him. The endurance of people in our lives encompasses the most difficult challenges we face, but our interaction with people also is the source of happiness and reasons for living. It all boils down to valuing each person our life touches by bringing them respect, joy, and, most of all, love.

Abiding Situations

Please Sir May I Have Another

Forced into the disability system by ALS, I entered the strange financial state of limited resources and governmental benefit which creates unnecessary burdens. It means relying on programs that frequently change on a whim depending on the way the political winds are blowing. Even added benefits cause uncertainty and confusion. When it involves medical care, the problems worsen. Medicare covers eighty percent of health care expenses and provides no caregiving aid while I make just enough over the Medicaid limit, where I cannot use the program. The constraints also mean when facing unexpected or significant expenses, it pushes our income beyond its limits.

Altogether, this creates the perfect financial storm. I earn an amount qualifying for the least help. It's not enough to make us independent. It hurts that my severe disability requires significant sums of money for the quality of life items beyond my health demands. It all adds up to one thing I never thought I would do, begging. Whether from family, friends, or strangers, the act pains me to my core each time I'm forced to beg. I put off personal needs as long as I can since I live on borrowed time. However, for Lisa and our daughters, I do whatever's necessary to provide the most normal life I can for them.

Today, the air conditioner went out. 2018 already was a blistering summer, and it is only July eighth. The so-called dog days of summer just started. The only saving grace keeping us from melting in this heat is, the day is less humid than typical in Missouri. However, the rest of the week, the humidity along with the temperatures are climbing with KY3 News predicting the heat index will exceed 105 degrees.

My condition makes me as sensitive to the heat as the cold. The only difference, getting hot, becomes dangerous. I don't sense I am overheating because I go from regular to my heart racing and realizing that I'm extraordinarily hot in an instant. Even playing football during the sweltering two-a-day practices in August, I never experienced overheating as I do now. My only gauge showing a potential problem comes from surrounding people, particularly Lisa.

Anymore, she's hot all the time, so it's more determining the level of her discomfort. The best indicator is when she says her boobs are sweating. I know it's childish, but every man deep down has that little boy inside them giggling and saying she said boobs. I tapped into this basic instinct providing myself a warning sign for overheating trouble.

The price of a new system falls into the category of beyond our means so, once again, I must seek help from others. Beg! The problem this time is I did a recent GoFundMe campaign for my personal needs. It's been twenty-five years since my diagnosis, so I outlived the usefulness of my equipment. I also developed severe dental issues since Medicare doesn't cover them, so I put it off because we couldn't afford my going to a dentist.

People blessed me with their generosity for that drive. How do I request more even though the immediate necessity of an air conditioning system is greater? All I can do is put my trust in God to provide an answer for my family, so when I release my worries and request help, money floods in answering our prayers.

Everyone goes through difficult financial situations in their lives. When it occurs, the uncertainty causes a faithful person to question if God will provide. When Jesus instructs us to not worry about such things because God provides for our needs, it might be one of the most challenging things a Christian does.

Trust composes our faith. Weakness and pride produce obstacles making the situations faced much worse. My journey with ALS taught me if I trust in God by humbling myself in that trust, He provides everything we need. Does it mean sitting back and God gives us whatever we want? No, God isn't a magical genie granting your wishes.

I work hard seeking solutions with His guidance, but when I hit a wall, I let God carry the burden smashing whatever is in my way. This realization means being thankful for what you receive and acknowledging what you don't need.

It means believing in yourself by doing the work required to move toward the path God sets before you. It means asking for help and accepting the generosity of others when needed. Ultimately, it means genuinely focusing on what's important in life, the lives you touch each day instead of material things which distract from your purpose.

The Handicapped Game

The one thing that's different about my life now than before being disabled by ALS is how I experience and interact with the physical world around me. In the next section, I delve into the more profound and darker aspects of what I endure. However, this section sums up the frustration felt but through humorous events from when I venture into the world outside of my home.

My brother, Greg, picked me up for a St. Louis Cardinals game at Busch Stadium, the place of some of my fondest and sacred childhood memories with my brother and dad. It seems appropriate that my first adventure out on a ventilator is to this special place. My three nephews come with us for the late afternoon game, but it isn't entirely for the generational family experience. My power wheelchair is a beast size wise. When they added a steel tray to hold my ventilator, the size of a small microwave, it became impossible to maneuver the wheelchair in the van, so I face forward. I now face the side of the van, affectionately christened Bucky by Lisa, because I can only back directly into it from the side entrance lift.

Besides having my view obstructed by the lift, every rapid stop or start causes my upper body to slide forward or back. My oldest nephew, Brent, is in the front seat to stop me going that way and my eight-year-old twin nephews, Matt and Nick, are in the back seat. In what becomes a rite of passage for Greg's kids and mine, we charge the twins with getting my head up since it's inevitable to fall over. I maintain no neck control in my wheelchair.

There isn't a handbook for going out on a ventilator, so we're in the trial-and-error stage. It would have been sooner, but between the vent tray install and the realization that my wheelchair locking system needed repositioning, it's been a year since I ventured out!

It takes Greg minutes into the drive to realize my new position in Bucky proves problematic. A red sports car cuts us off slamming on their brakes for a light that allows you to turn left if oncoming traffic allows. My upper body flies forward. My momentum only stops because of my wheelchair's lap belt and my head hitting the back of the driver's seat cracking my spine all the way down. I get wedged somehow between the arm of my wheelchair and the headrest of the van's seat where Brent, with the help of the twins, cannot get me upright. Greg pulls over to straighten me and make sure everything's all right.

Despite the inauspicious start to our day and my unexpected chiropractic adjustment, I'm no worse for the wear. The only problem becomes I need adjusting to be in a comfortable position, but I know that requires taking me out of the van to achieve. Even though I realize it means being uncomfortable and enduring pain until we get out at the stadium in about thirty minutes, I don't ask Greg to do anything. It's something I learned to do, balance my exact needs while trying not to put someone else out to get comfort.

I'm more aware of my need requests when out in my wheelchair since I realize it's much more difficult making the adjustments. The battle is between my pain threshold in what I can endure and how long I can endure because I can't move into a better position. It's a rare occasion when I'm comfortable in my wheelchair, and even then, it might last an hour.

By the time we reach the stadium area to find a parking place, I'm beyond my pain threshold. It's hard explaining the level of pain created by pressure points from not moving, but without hesitation, I contend nothing I experienced in my life compares to this agony. I broke bones, passed kidney stones, and had multiple surgeries. Each of those has moments of higher intensity, in my experience, it ebbs and flows, and they respond better to pain pills. Pressure from lack of movement is a different animal since the pain near equals the intensity of the other things mentioned. It's relentless while exponentially increasing over time as the pressure continues unabated. The nerves have road rage telling me to move already, not recognizing I need a tow truck to move.

Seeing or sensing my distress, Greg turns right instead of left as instructed when entering the parking garage for the full-sized, handicapped van area. Bucky is a behemoth that should stay in the big and tall section of the store not wondering wistfully about the petite part of the store. We're a little way in when something happens, BOOM followed by scrapping and a bump down as the rear of the van passes below a concrete beam. After my brother stops, the twins in unison express what the rest of us are thinking, "Whoa!!!"

When Greg and Brent get out to assess the damage and figure out what to do, it becomes clear the last bump worsened our predicament. The rear of Bucky is higher than the rest. Had Greg stopped before that portion got past the beam, he could have just backed out. Since he couldn't, we're stuck in no-mans-land between beams. Our choices are to deflate the back tires and try to back up or go forward, hoping it doesn't get lower and rip the top off. It's become a familiar scenario in my time with ALS, guessing which option is worse.

After Greg does recon making sure it doesn't get lower, we move forward not looking back and besides deflating the tires meant waiting for help which ruins our day. Life's too short to postpone for a perfect solution when you're hoping to create beautiful memories. Brent becomes a color commentator once we get started, "Dad, here comes a beam!" BOOM! However, it's the increasing laughter from the backseat that is a reminder from God, sometimes you sit back and enjoy the ride no matter how bumpy it gets.

The parking garage mishap is a metaphor for my ALS journey; I keep moving forward, knowing big bumps are coming. I learned to enjoy the time between the beams. If you experience troubles in life and you understand more are coming, don't waste the blissful periods worrying about what's next. Instead, embrace the happiness and love today brings. Revel in the miracle of life God gives you between the beams!

After finding an outdoor parking spot, I doubt Greg ever parks Bucky in a garage again. We unload. I get sweet relief by being adjusted. We're further from the stadium here, but I enjoy the "walk" anywhere since being in a wheelchair. When we go on the second block of the sidewalk, we discover there's no curb cut at the end for my wheelchair to continue. We must backtrack which fortunately we find a driveway about halfway down the block. This means my brother drives me down the street in game traffic while my nephews follow along on the walk. Greg must walk by my side to drive my wheelchair. It makes negotiating game traffic more difficult. We realize that the wheelchair controller by my right-hand needs to move behind me since I no longer drive myself.

As we get closer to Busch Stadium, we see brand new curb cuts which make us let down our guard to the challenges we've been facing already this trip. I notice the one inch or more lip as we cross one street to the next sidewalk which jostles me around going up it. I need adjusting once we get to the stadium. Now that the foot traffic picked up, I can't warn Greg to be wary of the lip size between the street and the curb cuts. He's busy navigating my wheelchair through the people, trying to not run over someone cutting in front of us. I'm along for the ride at this point.

With all the noise, it's a miracle to communicate with anyone. As a crowd of people surrounds us at the light for the next street crossing, it's impossible to see what lies ahead. I'm glad I don't suffer from claustrophobia because being so low in a crowd is a little disconcerting.

When the light turns for us to cross, my wheelchair suddenly flips forward, throwing me out except for the lap belt holding me in it. If not for Greg catching the handlebar at the head of my wheelchair, I would have hit the street with the weight of the chair on top of me. Later, he comments on how that could have killed me. I agree with his assessment.

It takes the kindness of another gentleman to get me upright and back on the sidewalk. That's when I realize I'm not breathing because a tube became disconnected during the commotion. It takes a few seconds for anyone to hear my ventilator alarming. At that point, I realize from Greg's first examination that the main breathing tube didn't disconnect. The problem is a small sensor tube disconnection. Uh-oh, it's a situation that might be beyond his experience of diagnosis.

While I can breathe with the tube off, in this situation with the small hose disconnected, I cannot breathe meaning within a few minutes; I will be in serious trouble. By the grace of God, Brent sees it disconnected the small tube. I don't know how long it took, but it's long enough I became concerned. The two incidents I experience within seconds of each other is a reminder of how close I walk on the edge of death now.

When my daughter, Kelsey, is ten, a similar disconnection occurs. Ironically, it's after a Cardinals game. She's calm and an expert with my care. The wheelchair barely stops before she corrects the problem in seconds. Kelsey impressed Greg and me seeing her quick action.

We make it to our seats without further death-defying occurrences. It's a sunny and warm September day. We're having a terrific time at the game. The only negative experience occurs when

I need to use the facilities. Greg takes me, but we must wait for the only accessible stall where my brother assists me using a urinal. It's not a situation you enjoy needing help with since it's an intimate moment. I released any discomfort or embarrassment about such cases long ago by training my mind to not think about the situation.

The delay waiting for a stall means we're there when the rush occurs between innings. It's something I desperately wanted to avoid. As the small bathroom fills with men, I see a guy who's drunk making a beeline toward me. He finished his business without washing his hands. He yammers how it's great I'm out. When he gets emotional about my physical state, he places both hands on my shoulders and leans over getting face-to-face. Greg sees my disgust at being assailed the way I am. He's gentle but firm getting the guy off me. To add insult to injury, a non-disabled man used the stall I needed. Lord, I appreciate my struggles can move people, but can't You move them to wash their hands first before violating my space.

The rest of the day goes off without a hitch except my twin nephews getting into a tussle. They cause a roar of laughter from the surrounding crowd. As we're leaving the stadium, I tell Greg to avoid that one section of sidewalk where I nearly dumped out of my wheelchair. He stays in the street. It seems odd to people seeing us doing it. One ass even honks his horn and yells for us "fucking morons" to get out of the street. We wish we could.

That's when I first hear the faint but distinct chirp, crackling sound that shows my ventilator battery power is getting low. That can't be since it's supposed to last a minimum of twelve hours. It's less than half that time. I only perceive it once before we get back to the van. I pray it was just a glitch. We're in traffic on Highway Forty when I hear it again. The chirping crackle is loud. Greg wonders out loud what the noise is. He doesn't realize a serious problem could unfold.

I cannot communicate with him well enough to tell him it's my vent, or we have approximately thirty minutes before the battery runs out. That's about how far we're from my house in the best circumstances. Lisa gave him a quick lesson on what to do when it happens, which means getting me out of the van for an outlet. It takes about five minutes for Greg to figure out my vent is making the noise, so I let him know we have thirty minutes before the vent stops. He speeds. We make it to the Chesterfield exit in record time coming from a game. Even with this good fortune, twenty-five minutes elapsed since the noise started. We still have ten to fifteen minutes driving to my house, where it takes five minutes getting into the house.

I notice my lungs seem tight. It feels like a chest cold when I breathed normally. Congestion on a ventilator is a whole different animal. The type experienced now is my lungs getting dry. Dryness can cause a mucus plug. I never encountered one. They explained to us it's like a big booger that kills you quickly if not addressed appropriately. The plug cuts off the lungs by clogging my breathing tube.

The dryness is making my vent work harder, which isn't ideal since the resulting lung tightness drains the battery faster. I can tell because the squealing sound is getting louder and is occurring on each breath given. It's making my brother panic somewhat. I pray it won't fail after each breath. Being caught at a red light is an eternity.

We make it to my house — what a relief. Lisa is now around. She knows what she's doing. My attention and concern turn to my breathing. I can't tell if it's the vent or my lungs or both. As we enter the house, my ventilator quits. By the grace of God, the battery held out over forty minutes. It's seconds before Lisa plugs the vent in.

The chaotic situation does not end though because my breathing difficulties weren't just limited to the battery running out. I struggle to get air in my lungs despite the vent being at full strength. After Greg and the boys say goodbye, Lisa notices how much I'm laboring with the air pressure getting high. I finally communicate with her that this problem is a dryness issue, so I need switching to my regular ventilator. It has a heated water humidifier connected to it. Within in minutes, I sense the relief of the tightness in my chest. With yet another crisis averted, I am exhausted from my crisis filled but fun day.

While Lisa prepares to move me to bed, Kelsey entertains me with tales of her adventures I missed during my outing. One advantage of ALS is that I have been around every moment of my precious daughter's life. Today's the first time, outside of my hospital stay for the tracheostomy, that Kelsey saw me leave and come home. We are laughing together when suddenly the vent cuts my breath off. That's weird.

Something broke off my lung and clogged my breathing tube causing ventilator alarms with each blow and releases because of the high pressure. I am not breathing! It's not a big concern since Lisa springs into action suctioning me to remove whatever is causing this issue. The suctioning machine is a miniature wet-vac that gets fluid out of your lungs. The same weakness that makes it where I cannot breathe also makes my cough ineffective. The suctioning procedure is not pleasant, but it's now routine for us and takes seconds.

As Lisa does the typical method, the suction catheter hits a wall. Instead of pulling out liquid nothing happens. No matter how forceful she is, the suction catheter won't go past the blockage as it should. This has never happened before. After thirty seconds, we both panic a little. Lisa moves onto the only thing she can do before completely removing the trache, which is an extreme desperation move.

Lisa removes what they call the inner cannula, a smaller, clear hard plastic tube within the breathing tube. A little piece of dried gunk comes out on the end which she cleans with a small bristle brush, essentially a pipe cleaner. After I'm still unable to breathe, doubt creeps into my mind. God, am I going to die here in front of my wife and daughter? Lisa has a few minutes to resolve the situation on her own, or I am dead.

My body is frantic for air, causing my heart to pound faster and faster. God help Lisa figure this out. She continues putting the cannula in and out, cleaning little pieces each time. Finally, a big wad comes out. The vent gives me the breath of life. My lungs take thirty more minutes to clear everything out and return to normal. My exhaustion feels like I ran a marathon. Thank God the clog didn't happen while I was with my brother. Greg doesn't possess the knowledge to assess the breathing issue. I would have perished.

We all face adverse situations to endure in life. They can come on suddenly without warning or have a slow, ominous buildup. The situations are brief or last years, and while they seem endless, they end. They try you physically, emotionally, mentally, and spiritually. Situations you endure shape all these aspects of your life. They mold your soul. They can even break you.

The thing to remember is, however devastating it may seem; you can use those times of dismay to style a better version of yourself in God's eyes. Just as iron and carbon combined through fire create steel, with God's help, you use the flame of situations endured to make a better and stronger you. What if a situation breaks you? Nothing remains impossibly broken with time, effort, and God.

Whenever you find yourself in trying, even impossible situations, lean on and pull strength from the spirit He placed in your soul.

Abiding Conditions

A condition, being diagnosed with ALS, forever alters your life. A fatal diagnosis and disability are the natural conditions we recognize. We empathize with them. There are many subtle conditions people suffer. They range from mental illness to victims of abuse to suffering the effects of a tragic event. In some ways, these conditions impacting a person's life are more difficult because no one sees their pain. When they do, they're ignored. Often the person dismisses their plight as trivial since others don't accept they're hurting. They give up.

A life-altering condition entering your life devastates you instantly. It continues to shape and change your life even after its initial damage. The unsolicited change becomes your new normal.

ALS destroyed the life I thought I would have the moment the doctors uttered the words, "You have ALS." After causing most of the physical destruction possible, Lou Gehrig's Disease continues to impact my life even though I've adjusted to its effects. Tomorrow, if God makes my body whole again, I will never escape ALS or its influence on my life.

I won't regain the life I once had. Honestly, I wouldn't want that life. The next chapter focuses on why I state this, but now I am telling you what I endure because of Lou Gehrig's Disease. It's not the focus of my daily life; however, to examine why we endure conditions as part of our existence. It is necessary to reveal my real suffering.

I already detailed the physical and financial impacts of my disease, and mostly, I accepted and overcame those limitations. Many people focus on my inability to walk, speak, and use my arms. It's tough adjusting to the loss of independence. However, the reality is once I reached the point of acceptance of my new dependent state, I rarely think about it in my daily life.

One reason for my ability to not focus on what ALS took from me centers on God packing in a full physical life before Lou Gehrig's Disease entered it. I competed in different sports; swam in two oceans; hiked one-hundred ten miles in the Rocky Mountains; worked with my hands; gave speeches in front of thousands. These are amongst the highlights before ALS entered my life. When I mourned the life taken from me, God brought me peace through this realization. I had done and experienced more in my shortened healthy physical life than many accomplish in a lifetime. Knowing children experience only physical disability in their lives humbles me at the richness of my life before ALS.

While I learned to accept my physical limitations, it doesn't mean I don't desire God's restoration of my former health. I pray for healing each day. That's not something I endure anymore. The most difficult challenges are not the obvious physical obstacles but lie in minor items you might not consider.

On a personal level, there's no solution for the lack of privacy using the toilet. It's hard enough to relieve yourself for strangers that are nurses, but the first time ALS forced me to rely on my wife to do it, I wept. Over time, I internalized the embarrassment and discomfort of requiring help. Eventually, I learned to let my mind not think about it. However, after twenty-one years, requiring help with toileting needs along with being fed like an infant, are the times each day, I cannot escape the devastating effects of ALS. This personal anguish is still far from the worst parts of my condition, torturing my soul.

Real pain lies in the inability to handle my part physically helping and supporting others, particularly my family. It's in my fiber to always pitch in and help whatever way I can because that's how my parents raised me. They even built everyday chores from lawn work to house cleaning into my DNA. The expectations of having a work ethic and helping are at my core, so being denied that by ALS lost a big chunk of who I am.

Each time my family moves since having ALS becomes a gut-wrenching experience. I sit and watch others doing the things I should be doing. Every so-called guy duty, no matter how small, done by Lisa and our daughters, reminds me of what I cannot do. It's a source of constant frustration. I aggravate them sometimes telling them what to do or how to do it, but it's hard to resist a basic instinct. If they knew many times, I fight the desire to give instructions and would happily do it myself; maybe it wouldn't aggravate them.

Sometimes my frustration from being permanently sidelined comes out in negative ways causing further regret of my situation. The annoyance isn't with my family but lies with my inability. The internal conflict between desiring to take care of things and my incapacity to do anything remains a constant source of consternation. This conflict isn't the worst issue endured from ALS.

Daddy, can you coach my team? Some variation of this theme occurred with my three daughters as they became old enough to recognize I differed from their friend's dads. I didn't expect how heartbreaking these moments would be. They are open wounds that pain me deeply. I recognize this ache never leaves. ALS denied me something I hold as a fundamental part of fatherhood. Worse, it deprived my children of the memories I cherish with my dad. It's impossible for me to reconcile the idealized childhood I had with my dad and what my daughters lost because of my disability.

I tried attending what I could during Kelsey's early years of activities. However, I realized that when I attended the focus went from her to the act of my attending. Lisa focused on my care instead of Kelsey. She didn't have either parent fully there for her. I decided it was best to stay at home so Lisa could give our daughters her full attention. My absence from these events was and continues to be distressing to endure. The solace I take is our children only know a home life with both parents always present. In today's world, it's normal for children having a world where both parents have work-life distractions.

The final, most challenging insult I must endure, my disability causes the inability to give affection. My children don't know about having a father who carries them on his shoulders, pushes them on a swing, wipes their tears or dances with them. The simple tasks of holding their hand, reading them a story, and hugging them are beyond my abilities.

The lowest and darkest times are when hurt, fright, or sadness overcomes Lisa and my girls. I cannot provide the comfort they need. I am supposed to be their refuge, their protector, their rock. God, why have you forsaken my body, so I can't be the man I desire to be? Why do I suffer the indignity of my disability when others don't seem to care or want to be good people? What did I do to suffer such a horrible fate? WHY AM I ENDURING THIS?

I won't attempt to assume the reasons I endure so much from having ALS applies to everyone. That would be presumptuous explaining away someone's painful experiences. Frankly, the tragedies many deal with are incomprehensible. I only speak for my endurance of ALS and what I believe is God's purpose for it. My hope is by sharing my understanding of suffering you find the answers to whatever you must abide in your life.

Lou Gehrig's Disease continues to shift and shape the focus of what has importance in my life. When I was well, it was easy falling into the trap of pursuing success and possessions as central goals for life. Even with a solid foundation of values instilled in me by family, I succumbed to false promises. Our society bombarded me with the message that the measuring stick for a valuable existence lives in wealth, power, and beauty. It claims possessing these things creates the road to happiness. This was before social media was promoting these messages.

Few achieve the perfection projected. Even then, most discover empty, unfulfilling lives at the end of the rainbow, not the promised pot of gold. When I lost the possibility of possessing any of those things, God revealed where the value in this precious life lies. With each physical loss, I learned I grew mentally, emotionally, and spiritually. The transformation was hard. It took time to understand what's unique in life, changing my soul.

The things I miss aren't the things I possess or even my physical appearance. What I crave is the ability to interact with the surrounding people. My having ALS taught me what to value and prioritize in life: family, friends, love, and God. The disease humbles me of vanity and makes me see how senseless it is concentrating on outward beauty. I am forced to look inward by disability and focus on making myself a better man through reflection and growth in that realm. Once I emerged from the cocoon where I transitioned from normalcy to disabled; I discovered a better and stronger man.

God uses each instance I endure to shape me into a superior version. It wasn't until I quit resisting these changes and released my anger over what I lost and continued to experience that I understood God's higher purpose for me. I now realize that wealth, power, and beauty are the measuring stick of a life well lived. Modern culture defines them incorrectly. Seek a wealth of love. Accept the power of God's grace. Find beauty in people's souls.

I discovered this truth through the endurance of ALS and the severe disability it caused. Through weakness, I found tremendous strength. With God, nothing is impossible. My prayer is you don't have to abide by severe conditions to gain this knowledge, but, if you do, you gain insight from my journey.

I'm all right with weaknesses, insults, disasters, harassments, and stressful situations for the sake of Christ, because when I'm weak, then I'm strong.

2 Corinthians 12:10

7

A BLESSED LIFE

Those who stand firm during testing are blessed. They are tried and true.
They will receive the life God has promised to
those who love him as their reward.

James 1:12

One of the common themes surrounding my journey with ALS, I'm called a hero or held up as someone admired for the obstacles I overcome. The praise humbles my soul. I am just Jeff, a son, a brother, a husband, a father, and a friend making the best life like everyone else in this world. We all have problems and struggles; mine are more visible because I have ALS.

My daily life appears daunting. People believe they couldn't handle my condition. However, I grasp the God-given strength we all possess. More importantly, I gained the gift of sight. I see the multitude of blessings God gives me in my two lives, before ALS, and with ALS.

It's vital for each of us to recognize the blessings in our lives because they lay the bedrock in this world. By focusing on blessings, not on the storms and mountains we face, we don't get sucked into a vortex of negativity. The attention toward how God blesses us strengthens us, enables us to endure more, and ultimately leads us to a happy and fulfilling life journey.

Count your blessings may be a trite expression for some, but if practiced every day, it's a powerful tool for taking control of your life. It creates power within my spirit. I continue to use it for overpowering what seem insurmountable obstacles for many. I'm a blessed simple man.

Blessings for ALS

I'll show what it's like when someone comes to me, hears my words, and puts them into practice. It's like a person building a house by digging deep and laying the foundation on bedrock. When the flood came, the rising water smashed against that house, but the water couldn't shake the house because it was well built.

Luke 6:47-48

My elementary school years were challenging from a social standpoint. It began with my second-grade teacher, who by any standard, abused the boys in her class. She would paddle us for a minor infraction of her rules, but that was nothing compared to the emotional abuse she heaped on us. The teacher jerked us by our arms to the coat closet, which resulted in a verbal dressing down composed of assaults on your intelligence and appearance. Anything she could do to beat us down, she did.

In my case, besides those attacks, she told me over and over I would "kill" other boys if I fought with them because I was bigger. This declaration set me up for scorn and bullying when I wouldn't engage in tussles frequent for boys in the seventies. My second-grade year, I put on weight because of the situation created by my teacher. I then faced additional ridicule as a fat kid since I ate my feelings. School days were my personal hell.

Being bullied in elementary school because of an abusive second-grade teacher is a blessing? In my case, yes. God helped me survive this period without falling into a failure spiral by providing loving and caring parents. They made sure moving forward that I had equally supportive teachers. My parents allowed me to emerge relatively unscathed from a difficult period in my life. They ensured this, in part, by getting me into the third-grade class of an incredible teacher, Mrs. Ruth Vaughan. She rebuilt my trust in teachers and helped me love school again.

The problem was, I never told my parents the whole story about what the teacher had done until I was in the sixth grade. It's the year organized football started, the sport I loved. Football started my desire to train to be in better shape to compete. Training with my dad at the high school football field where I would one day play turned into much more.

Dad took the opportunity to get me to reveal the issues I was having. He did it the whole time, but this instance clicked with me. I unburdened myself of all I carried. He encouraged me to stand up for myself, not to seek a fight but defend myself if someone challenged me. He reassured me he witnessed me holding my own with my older brother so that I could persevere. The next few years, I found the principal's office several times for fighting. I took licks with the paddle in front of my foe when they chose detention. It became a badge of honor although I realize today it's viewed as physical abuse.

More critical during my sessions with Dad, he told me that God was preparing me for something bigger than me. One night when I became exhausted from running bleachers at the stadium, he sat me down and put his arm around my shoulder. It was a dark, warm night. The sky clear with the stars shining bright. A father and son picturesque moment. He told me how proud he was of me for overcoming the challenges I faced. A son can get no better compliment than making his father proud. Then he told me something that's seared into my memory. He said, "Son, I believe God has great plans for you. I don't know what it is, but I believe you will do something special with your life." Dad was right.

God prepared me for more significant challenges and to be His instrument, helping others understand His grace in our lives. That period taught me to persevere through difficult circumstances. Always remain positive even when things turn seriously bleak. Life is not fair, so put your head down and trudge forward when you ache to give up and quit. I learned these lessons at a young age, which toughened and strengthened me for more significant challenges ahead.

Blessings in life aren't necessarily obvious or pleasant at the time they occur. Often it takes life experience to understand something's purpose and how it blessed not cursed your life. God prepares us for burdens beyond the horizon.

The story of my school struggles represents one of many that prepared me for a journey with ALS. Some were defeats or struggles, but the vast majority were victories and memorable moments. I mentioned before I experienced more than many achieve in my healthy twenty-six years. Some think my active life should leave me longing to continue living that way. Part of me still mourns that loss. It's centered on my inability to create new memories with my wife and daughters. God gave me another viewpoint. Overall, I pull strength from my former physical life, knowing one day I will enjoy those things in this life or the next. I will achieve fulfillment.

Much more significant than my previous physical fulfillment occurred with God's gift of surrounding me with a remarkable family, friends, teachers, coaches, and mentors during my formative years. They helped build a foundation that's so strong it withstands anything. They made me with care through love, support, faith, and teaching me what's fundamental and valuable. This groundwork allowed me to take on the worst ALS threw at me. With God's guidance and help, I emerged a better man.

Two incredible and generous God-given parents made me that way. Dad taught me what it means to be a man, how to persevere in the face of harsh conditions. He continues to serve as my compass in life. Dad was my best friend while maintaining his authority of a loving father. Mom provided unconditional love and support throughout my childhood. She created a home that was so secure and loving it would be the envy of television families portrayed in the sixties and seventies. She stayed involved and supportive of every activity her children chose. After Dad's death, Mom transformed herself into a working woman providing a fantastic example of changing yourself and overcoming unexpected changes. With parents like these, God set me up to excel under the worst circumstance life would throw at me.

Blessings Because of ALS

I know the experience of being in need and of having more than enough;
I have learned the secret to being content in any and every circumstance,
whether full or hungry or whether having plenty or being poor.
I can endure all these things through the power
of the one who gives me strength.

Philippians 4:12-13

As impossible as it seems, ALS benefited my life. It created positive experiences I wouldn't encounter otherwise. It made me a better man. I realize my expressing this opinion upsets some with Lou Gehrig's Disease, especially those newly diagnosed. I understand and respect their view that ALS generates nothing but pain, heartache, ruin, and terror.

It took years to embrace a different prism through which to view our shared disease and disability. Some see their families torn apart, their lifetime of work shattered. They lose everything, including their faith in God. I don't express the blessing of ALS lightly because I admit the good fortune I realize in many aspects of my particular battle with Lou Gehrig's Disease.

When ALS forced me into disability retirement, I mourned not working. In an old school mindset, I believe you work until you can't physically. I witnessed generations of Lester men provide this example. Both my grandfather and great-grandfather stayed engaged with their small business until their late eighties. However, a unique benefit occurred from my disability; I witnessed my daughter's lives like I never would observe without ALS. I was home for the entirety of their childhood, sharing countless joyous and

114

momentous events. Many between their birth and starting school, I would have missed without ALS invading my life.

For my daughters, they never knew a home without both parents there. In an age when both parents need to work, it's a rare experience, so it's a blessing given to my family from God because of my disability. How you frame your circumstances forms your perspective.

The trials of Lou Gehrig's Disease formed and refined me like when Michelangelo took a discarded piece of marble, turning it into David. ALS discarded my life, a new work in progress, with my devastating diagnosis. Everyone assumed my life was over, including me for a while. God had other plans.

The struggles changed my outlook and focus. Slowly, I realized I would survive and thrive while becoming a better version of myself, but I'm not suggesting I became the perfection David represents. No one is. I am just a more refined version who's still evolving. I understand what to value in this world and why we exist drives me, so I recognize the daily mistakes which I make while trying to improve too. It's a never-ending process of evolving.

If you stop attempting to better yourself this way, your soul dies from lack of attention. You become a bitter shell of flesh with nothing but darkness inside. Learning forgiveness for what I perceive as wrongs done against me and more so forgiving my shortcomings brings me closer to God's desire for us.

I realize now what a waste of time and effort it is to pursue things society tells us we should chase. When you listen to most who have achieved wealth, fame, or power, they weren't directly pursuing those things. They reached them by following their passion, and those things were a byproduct of that pursuit. I learned to be happy and content with what I have and not make myself miserable with what I don't.

I believe God used my disease and disability to teach me what life means. He now uses me as His instrument showing others. That road leads to a happy and fulfilling life.

With Friends Like These

Therefore, as God's chosen, holy and loved, put on compassion, kindness, humility, gentleness, and patience. Be tolerant with each other and, if someone has a complaint against anyone, forgive each other. As the Lord forgave you, so also forgive each other. And over all these things put on love, which is the perfect bond of unity.

Colossians 3:12-14

The generosity of a boundless human spirit casts a long shadow of comforting shade for anyone weary from a long trek in the beating sun. It heals what medicine can't. The oasis of love gives someone struggling with burdens too heavy to bear alone a rest from their troubles. It's the central message of God's call for us. We are each supposed to be an oasis, so if everyone answers His call, the desert of despair disappears. Aiding someone answers Jesus' command to love your neighbor.

When healthy, I received love, support, and kindness that was plentiful. It wasn't until I lost everything that I witnessed goodness beyond imagination. Perhaps I appreciated kind gestures more, but I believe my condition allowed people to open their hearts in ways they don't allow themselves outside their close circle.

In the beginning, their support grew from pity. Over time, as my story changed and emerged from my death sentence, people embraced me tighter. I receive love and support in countless ways, big and small from friends, acquaintances, and strangers. Their gifts humble me. It's how God wants us to treat everyone our lives touch: no exception. I count it amongst the greatest blessings received in my life, love revealed in its pure form.

Like anyone, I get disappointed by people just as I'm sure my actions sometimes upset others. There are a few instances where so-called friends have tried to take advantage of my situation for money or self-glory. Compared to many with ALS, I avoided the worst scenarios of neglect, abuse, conflict, revenge, and divorce. There are horrific stories that shattered families. It shredded the person's dignity well beyond the ravaged body ALS caused.

God blessed me. I didn't experience the worst aspects of ALS on my relationships. I will never understand why He spared me since my positive experiences outweigh the negative a thousand to one. What I discovered when unfortunate events happen to give and seek forgiveness then move on and separate from the person if it's required. Don't waste seconds letting negativity steal your attention, your joy.

Ice Buckets from Heaven

What happens when you exceed the devastating prognosis of Lou Gehrig's Disease by fifteen to twenty years? You celebrate each day as a blessed gift from God, hoping you live in a way honoring the extra time you're given. It's how we should live regardless of our health since we live happier, more fulfilling lives. As Tim McGraw opines in song, live like you're dying otherwise when you get a disease like mine, you're not free to live.

That's a recipe for regret.

My longevity also has a downside. I'm outliving costly equipment. It's my wheelchair accessible van, which is the biggest concern. Bucky, my van so named by Lisa, has seen better days. After twenty years, rust and peeling paint are Bucky's main appearance features. Mechanically, things are so bad it's no longer reliable other than outings in town, and soon it won't achieve that. We can't afford the significant expense of buying a replacement van. I face the real possibility of becoming homebound.

Trying to be proactive and not become a victim of my condition, I started GoFundMe to offset the cost and figure out the rest later. God provided many times before. I learned patience putting trust in Him to unfold unknown possibilities for me.

The biggest show of support was when I started a social media drive to attend my graduation in Michigan. What began as a longshot attempt to grab attention from a television show took on a life of its own. A huge fundraising event, Lester Launch, in my hometown of Sikeston, raised a considerable amount. When local media stories gained national coverage in USA Today, the donations were vast. Family, friends, and strangers offered bountiful support in both time and money. It allowed me and my entire family to attend my graduation. I cannot imagine anything close to that happening again.

After several months using GoFundMe, I received a generous amount of donations to replace Bucky, but it's not near enough. God, I understand you always deliver so maybe I don't need a van anymore. Is He sending me a subtle message that my time on earth is coming soon? I shouldn't let such thoughts come to mind, but with my health on the edge of a cliff, I cannot help it. Most times, I focus on today; otherwise, the lingering doubt hanging over my life consumes me.

An incredible turn of events this summer brought amazing hope and awareness to the ALS community. They call it the ALS Ice Bucket Challenge. It went viral on social media. Outside a star's diagnosis of ALS, Stephen Hawking or the yearly Jerry Lewis MDA Telethon, ALS gets little media attention. However, this viral awareness dramatically changed that reality. People are taking videos of ice water dumped on their heads. Some are creative. The ice reactions are hilarious. What gives it a special touch is the dedications to people with ALS. It shows most people have someone they know who has Lou Gehrig's Disease, proving it touches more people than we thought. I'm flattered when friends dedicate their challenges honoring me. It's humbling.

Then it happens, someone suggests the help go to my Bucky campaign. It's hard accepting personal gifts for something benefiting ALS organizations. Despite my hesitation, it takes off like wildfire. My friends and family recruit everyone connected with them on Facebook. On some days, most of my day is happily watching videos dedicated to replacing Bucky honoring my ALS struggle and thanking people for their humbling gestures. Donations on GoFundMe explode. I'm halfway to the estimated cost when things calm down.

One challenge posted was from my church's youth group dedicated in my honor and Karen Hopkins' brother, who also has ALS. The Hopkins are good family friends besides being members of Lebanon First United Methodist Church. Besides seeing kids, I know including my daughter, Emily, along with Karen get doused with frigid ice water on my behalf, it brings a significant impact on my Bucky campaign. Our church becomes inspired. They pick up the mantle of my cause just as it appears to be winding down.

Through the fall and holiday season, they hold fundraisers and take a special collection on my behalf to cover the rest needed for a newer accessible van. The fundraising efforts exceed my graduation fundraiser, which I thought impossible. God shares His grace even though I had doubts. This reaffirms anything is possible with Him by your side.

I write about the blessings of friendship because that connects each of us. It's what unifies us regardless of whatever insignificant differences we have. The spirit of friendship allows people who were enemies during wars to embrace later in forgiveness. Friendship is the shared bond making each person, in this world, your brother and sister.

We should ground friendship in goodness and love, which is the foundation of what Jesus said is the greatest commandment to keep. I have seen and received so much from my friendship blessings, especially during my time with ALS. To use the words of Lou Gehrig, I'm the luckiest man alive because of the wealth of love I receive from friends.

Gifts from God

A good tree doesn't produce bad fruit, nor does a bad tree produce good fruit. Each tree is known by its own fruit.

Luke 6:43-44

Family is Everything

When beginning my journey with ALS, the greatest disappointment felt was being denied the blessing of having a family of my own. It's something I took for granted. I would be a husband and father. The experience of love and joy through both good times and bad was the expectation built within me. The family remains a cornerstone of a life well lived. It's a core belief I hold dear. A cruel twist of fate deprives me this destiny or, so I thought. ALS didn't deny me a family. It helped me appreciate the blessed gift of having a wife and children.

When we started our family with Kelsey's birth, I did not understand how much of her life I would witness. The brutal truth is I doubted I would impact her. I would become a phantom figure relegated in her memory to a few pictures and videos where we were together. Doubt causes one of the cruelest mind games of ALS since it's difficult expecting anything but further physical decline and your quick demise.

The fact was especially true in the mid-1990s with the internet in its infancy and not knowing what information you could trust. Lou Gehrig's Disease was emerging from its dark ages when someone became isolated after their diagnosis. The loneliness felt before technology was ruthless. During that period of gaining knowledge about ALS and its real effects, my progression always changed how I accessed my computer. ALS dramatically shrunk what I did independently. We wasted time figuring out how to adjust for the most basic task with Lisa's help. I could not spend my precious time researching. I needed to live in the moment with my family. The pre-Google and social media era meant searching was time-consuming. It was a tight-rope balancing act.

Fortunately for me, each day with a newborn is momentous, and I was there experiencing them with Kelsey. I would be around for her first birthday, but past that was uncertain even doubtful, so after Kelsey's birthday, each event I thought it might be my last. It made me stop looking beyond the next milestone and live for today. I cherished every day with my little girl.

In 1997, we celebrated Kelsey's second birthday then traveled to Washington, DC, for my sister's graduation from Georgetown Law School. I knew these would be my last major events besides holidays unless I went on a vent. The long trip took its toll on me and being carried up steps for Laura's graduation party brought home how severe my disability was becoming. That awareness didn't lessen the trip; instead, it caused me to savor each moment, but I did not realize then that graduations were milestones I would see for Kelsey.

I survived for many more key events from weddings to funerals to unexpected births of two additional daughters. Each major event was a gift from God. When I was there for Kelsey's graduation from high school as the valedictorian, the ceremony became a watershed moment. I allowed myself to entertain the belief I might be around for her graduation from Missouri State University where I graduated. It was the first time since her first birthday I allowed myself to think beyond my current circumstances. I still knew ALS could end my life, but I planned on being there for her next graduation.

When I got to March before her graduation from MSU in May, we planned for the excursion since it's in Springfield, about an hour away. A day trip isn't difficult given my condition. This is Kelsey's special day with family coming so we don't want my health to impact her day. We're extra cautious planning it. Lisa discovers my wheelchair batteries died since my fiftieth birthday outing to Springfield last October. It's no big deal since we replaced them multiple times over the years using the MDA's equipment program. The wheelchair becomes a more significant issue when I discover my local MDA discontinued their equipment program. It's a more tough process, but with Medicare paying the majority, it's an unnecessary pain more than anything.

When Lisa calls, she finds out that the process is near impossible to resolve before Kelsey's ceremony. The supply company insists I come in for a review before Medicare pays for the batteries. We got my chair without Medicare help. I won it writing an essay. Now they say I must prove I need one. The theme of showing I have advanced ALS produces infuriating scenarios for getting equipment. Lou Gehrig's Disease doesn't improve.

My disability has been severe for twenty years, yet each time we're required to prove it. This case creates a catch twenty-two. I cannot go anywhere without my wheelchair, but I am required to go in for the battery replacement for Medicare to pay. Lisa gets upset when multiple people can't grasp the absurdity of the situation and keep pushing for her to bring me in for the evaluation. They don't understand my advanced disability or the fact I am on a ventilator, so it's an undertaking for me to go out in my power wheelchair. It's yet another example of the unnecessary and ridiculous trials created for people with disabilities.

After not finding a resolution to the problem through the regular ALS groups, our frustration grows. I post about our mess on Facebook while asking God for a solution. It throws the floodgates open as blessings come pouring in to help. It comes from friends and strangers. Susan Woolner, who I barely know, takes on finding a solution for getting new batteries. A grant from the Susan Mast ALS Foundation quickly resolves the problem. Once again, I'm stunned by the generous spirit aimed toward me as God takes care of issues as small as this. It doesn't matter the insignificance. His love lifts us up. It's not lost on me the countless moments God intervened to bring my life to celebrate this special day of achievement for Kelsey. Even a tornado warning sounding as we leave the graduation doesn't diminish the day's perfection. The drenching rain entering Olive Garden for a celebration dinner with family served as a reminder of all the devastating storms, I made it through to see this special day.

I'm bursting with pride for Kelsey's accomplishments and with joy at God's blessing me to see them.

Milestones like these are special, regardless. When doctors alleged you weren't having children or live long enough to experience many, they gain special meaning. I appreciate each event as the God-given gifts. As tremendous as each milestone celebrated with my daughters is, they pale compared to the little moments which fill my heart with love and happiness. Giggling and laughter filling our home, excitement from successes, and even the letdowns or clashes that happen in a family makes life richer and fuller.

Helping our daughters grow into strong, bright, driven, spiritual young women who possess equal inward and outward beauty is the greatest accomplishment of my life. My legacy is secure because God gave me the blessing of being a father of daughters. I have the honor to guide and love them.

My Surprise Fiftieth Birthday Gift – January 28, 2017

When I turned fifty last October, I thought I reached the final major milestone supposedly denied by ALS. Marriage, children, a master's degree, and getting to an age where my peers also face their mortality are the major life events it should have denied. I beat ALS. Everything related to having children, their achievements, including having grandchildren, was beyond imagination when they diagnosed me with Lou Gehrig's Disease. I now believe I'm in the bonus rounds of life.

In late January, getting ready for bed, I checked my messages on Facebook. I hadn't checked them for several days despite seeing the red notification declaring there were new ones. It's when I first see a name that permanently changes my life, Jessica Thomas. This woman claims I am her biological father!

My initial reaction to someone telling me that, what scam are they running? I only have three daughters with my wife of twenty-two years. About to delete the message something catches my eye, AncestryDNA. That's easy enough to verify. I did the AncestryDNA test several years ago as a Christmas gift from my daughters to deepen my understanding of my genealogy research. My hope was it would break some walls in family lines my research hit.

The results I received pleased me because they allowed a breakthrough on my Lester line, which was a wall going back forty years to my Great Aunt Martha's research. I took a break from my genealogy research last November, so I was ignoring emails from Ancestry, knowing I would catch up whenever I started my research again in 2017.

Imagine my utter shock when I logged onto AncestryDNA, and it listed Jessica as my daughter with 100% confidence! I have a 32-year-old daughter come into my life a few months after my 50th birthday. I immediately responded, even though I was in shock. It's obvious my lack of response frustrated Jessica. The adoption officials told her parents I was aware and gave away my parental rights. Unfortunately, no one told me they were possibly pregnant when I was in high school. Jessica was conceived a month or two before my seventeenth birthday.

I say, unfortunately, because my parents raised me to take responsibility for any consequences of my actions so my family and I would have supported Jessica and her biological mother. This happenstance of finding Jessica equates to other fantastic events in my life, my marriage, and the birth of my three daughters. I got a daughter along with a son-in-law and three granddaughters!

There are several aspects of our connection story that make it miraculous. Since no one told me they were pregnant with my child,

I was not looking out for an adopted child or a kid raised by their biological mother. The fact I'm into genealogy is the reason I took the DNA test to find out my genetic heritage, which is the only reason my daughter found me. This became clear as Jessica, and I embarked on a quest finding her unknown biological mother. While discovering who it was and from the facts we had, we find out they didn't list me as the biological father on her original birth certificate. Jessica was born and adopted in Indiana. I am from Missouri. When Jess gets her original birth certificate if not for us both taking the AncestryDNA test, she would have never found me.

The biggest reason our connection is miraculous? Doctors predicted I wouldn't be alive. When I turned fifty last October, I felt what a blessed life I achieved by being determined not to give in to ALS. Little did I realize my tenacity living life on my terms would reveal such a special secret. God suddenly blessed my life with another beautiful and amazing daughter.

I understand the negative impact of surprising DNA findings. I helped Jess find her birth mother. She rejected Jess fearing the revelation of her secret. It is sad our society continues to brand people with a scarlet letter for adoptions. We should revel it as a source of joy. Even if the original act wasn't ideal, a child was born.

We found that despite the DNA proof and our desire to correct it, Indiana won't change Jessica's birth record. Their laws refuse listing me as the father. It bothers me the official record is forever wrong. The state said once Jessica's adoption was official, her original birth certificate was closed and cannot change. I understand protecting adoptive families. Our case won't affect them. It's upsetting that Indiana is officially keeping a lie in the face of indisputable evidence. The correction doesn't change the adoption. It's correcting the historical record. It rights the wrong for my being denied the chance as Jessica's father. They can reward family and love.

When you live through the challenges I have, you learn guilt and shame are wasteful emotions to internalize and avoid them because you miss out on so much. It's better to shine a light on them and make amends if needed. With a youthful indiscretion resulting in a child whether or not you knew, there should be no shame. We need to shed the scarlet letter syndrome that surrounds adoption. Even difficult situations when a child results from an affair, the child doesn't care.

My dad taught me being a man, a real man, means standing up and taking responsibility for your actions. He taught me by example that for your children, one word should guide you, love. Regardless, how and when Jess came into my life, it doesn't change she's my child and a part of me. I hope all my children know that despite any mistakes I made; they had a dad who loved them deeply. Nothing matters beyond that.

The experience of getting to know Jessica has been so positive it's like a dream scenario. We discovered many things we share in common both personality wise and physical traits. Even without the DNA match, it's impossible to deny Jessica is my child. Each day becomes an incredible journey of discovery deepening the bond of love we share. She stole a spot in my heart I didn't realize it had. I cannot imagine my life without her.

Jess ended up with the parents God wanted her to have. For their love, I'm forever grateful to them for making Jess the woman she is today. I never want to replace them but give Jess some added love in her life because we all could use that. I deeply appreciate the blessing received from living long enough to meet Jess. The significance of having her family be a part of my life isn't lost on me. A simple test brought love into my life and completed my family in such a beautiful way. It's beyond my wildest dream.

The Real Heroine

My story of triumph over the impossible odds given with the ALS diagnosis and the insurmountable obstacles it created for my life would not happen without Lisa. God's infinite blessing was His most meaningful gift given me by bringing such a woman of indomitable spirit into my life. Little did I realize He was guiding me before my life's journey took a dramatic turn. It proves God's resolute promise the moment He gave Lisa as a partner to overcome the monster trying to crush me. All blessings that came afterward lead back to her.

Without Lisa, my death occurred decades ago. She gave me reasons to fight and live for tomorrow. In giving me these motives, it allowed me to re-focus on why I am here and find my deeper purpose. She married me a year after my ALS diagnosis, has been my only caregiver since 1997, and gave me three incredible daughters while helping to create a home free of ALS. Despite my disability, we maintain a relatively normal loving relationship — another example of ALS' failure to destroy my life because of Lisa. Her love and care allow me to be free of my limitations and serve God's intentions for my life.

The circumstances and trials we faced together would destroy most people ten times over by now. I recognize it because in my twenty-five years with ALS; I observed countless friends with Lou Gehrig's Disease have their relationships and families utterly destroyed. God blessed me the day He brought the strongest woman I ever knew into my life.

Lisa provides the best example of love. She picked me up when I was at my lowest telling me together; we would move forward on an unknown path. We faced the fury of Lou Gehrig's Disease, where she didn't flinch. Sure, each of us has our moments of weakness, but we help each other by becoming stronger when the other is weak. We also have our moments as a couple as everyone does amongst the difficulties ALS causes. It has nearly broken us. In those times of strife, our relationship based in love strengthens us bringing us back together. Neither of us is perfect, but God united us, creating a perfect union greater than the separate parts.

She doesn't enjoy attention for the amazing, beautiful woman she is, both as a wife and a mom. Lisa is the force behind everything I do now. She is the cog of our family. Lisa is my greatest blessing, and she's the real heroine of my story. God gave me a real-life Wonder Woman!

Twenty-five Years and Counting

On October 1, 2018, I celebrated the twenty-fifth anniversary of my diagnosis. Some question, why would Jeff celebrate what's amongst the worst days of his life? That's a great question. I didn't celebrate Lou Gehrig's Disease devastating the life I knew and was planning on having. The words "You have ALS" shattered that life beyond repair. It meant I would become physically dependent even for the most basic needs we take for granted.

I endured indignities and embarrassment beyond imagination that permanently breaks some. Sometimes it broke me. Some people encouraged and excused my giving up and accepting my horrible fate at various points along my journey. While I recognize the difficulties, I face, it doesn't define my life and the man I became.

I celebrate rising from the ashes of my previous life like the mythical Phoenix. I rejoice in taking the road not taken by following my heart and trusting God leading my life to a better place. Doing this allows me to discover and understand what Jesus meant when He taught us that to follow Him is a rougher path, but it leads to greater glory. I revel at defying the odds and proving the naysayers wrong.

I celebrate all the victories, some losses, and especially the host of blessings I receive because I listened to God by not quitting. My successes include being awarded the MDA Person of the Year by the Missouri governor. Another feat was graduating from the University of Michigan-Dearborn. Both are pinnacles of my personal life. They happened after ALS did its worst damage. These triumphs rewarded my tenacity. God gave me this.

I mourn the lives of friends like Mark, Dave, Scott, Sarge, and so many others who battled Lou Gehrig's Disease with me but succumbed to it. Today, I lift them up and celebrate their lives.

I celebrate and praise God for the new life He gave me after my ALS diagnosis. He gave me the spirit to understand nothing is impossible with Him. God gave me such an abundance of love and support from family, friends, and strangers, making me truly a wealthy man. With everything He gives me, without reservation, I exclaim, "I am the luckiest man alive!"

A thief called ALS took nearly everything from me, including my life. I believe that even though I lost much, I gained so much more. I learned the real value in life: family, friendship, my spirit, my faith, and love. Nothing can steal those from me. Awareness of our blessings in life is a powerful tool for us to use. Acknowledging them as God-given gifts gives both strength and peace to your soul, bringing you closer to God's love and grace.

*Reflect upon your present blessings -- of which every man has many –
not on your past misfortunes, of which all men have some.*

Charles Dickens from A Christmas Carol and Other Christmas Writings

SECTION 3

LESSONS LEARNED

A tous les temps, a tous les peuples.

For all times, for all people.

The quote above is the guiding principle of scientists who work toward a universal unit of measure that's consistent throughout time and space providing certainty for all who use it. My journey with ALS taught me some fundamental truths I believe are essential for a life well lived. The universal measure of a good life.

This final section is the lessons I have learned on how to live your best life no matter your circumstances. I believe anyone will benefit reading this section either from the advice given or a change of perspective.

I don't pretend to have answers for all the problems people face in their lives since I probably don't know most of the questions. The following is what I found essential to living a happy and fulfilling life when it's stripped of extraneous things. It creates a guide for a purposeful journey. It provides a significant reason for God bringing us together.

8

CONTROL YOUR OWN DESTINY

This above all: to thine own self be true
And it must follow, as the night the day
Thou canst not then be false to any man

William Shakespeare: In Act 1, Scene III of Hamlet

One guide that helped me overcome ALS: listen to my heart before any other person's opinion about my circumstances. I believe it grounds me in God's guidance.

My parents raised me to depend on my own thoughts and beliefs based on gathering the best information available. It's severely tested when something serious like ALS enters your life because the destruction it brings along with uncertainty and fear of the unknown strips away your self-confidence. It also brings many uninformed views based on people's fears coming your way. The swirl of confusion and unsolicited advice overwhelms you.

The certainty of professional medical advice gives you a rock to grasp onto as you drown, but I learned medical advice includes the same fear bias as everyone else. In some ways, it's worse because they experience the worst aspects of my disease or something similar in a hospital setting. They project the reality at home would be worse. They cannot fathom someone without medical training performing better than them. The truth, many easily exceed their care. Lisa does. What I discovered; I was correct in taking a road not traveled because I listened to people with direct experience living with ALS often against "professional" advice. I followed my heart, which ended up taking me to places I didn't dream of going. It led me to a happy and fulfilling life.

My doctor's tale equates to people in your life who hold a power position requiring respect in your mind whether or not it's earned. Family, friends, teachers, preachers, and other authority or parental figures can guide you wrong even denigrate your goals and dreams. They can come from the most well-intentioned, loving places and still create severe damage to your life. You don't know what fear or experience motivates their opinion for your life.

When advice is driven by bad or even evil intentions toward you, the devastation can be substantial and take the rest of your life if allowed to control you. Their good, bad, and ugly intents hurt you. That only happens if you follow their lead. It's why listening to your heart and trusting it in the face of negative feedback must serve as your compass.

Does it mean ignoring outside input on what to do and useful information? No, you give everything careful thought revealing if God nudged you in a direction using someone else. I found you sense you're going against the way your heart wants and when people are guiding you correctly. Tenacity is positive when following what nourishes your soul. Stubbornness leads you to dark places if you merely do something resisting someone's advice.

Maybe a person constantly disrespects you, and you take their opinions with a grain of salt, but if the warning rings true, pause and consider heeding it. Prove to yourself their counsel is false. Appreciate that tenacity and stubbornness are different sides of the same coin, so it's easy going from tenacious self-advocate to becoming a stubborn mule.

The worst choices: blindly following what someone opinion, ignoring your better instincts or becoming frozen, not choosing a path. The first gives away your life, and the second causes you to be stagnant and die even if you're alive. Both lead you to unsatisfying and unhappy lives.

Staying true to yourself while seeking the best opinions and facts generates the balance you desire in finding the path God wants you to take. Always remember if you take a wrong turn, God is there helping you back where you need to go. Sometimes it means accepting help from others and humbling yourself, but it's never against what you know is right. Don't view yourself as a passenger. Be God's copilot steering your life where it needs to go.

In the same way, if you find yourself in a position offering advice, try giving it from your heart. Realize you have different strengths and skills than someone else, so your plan doesn't fit them. It's their life's journey, not yours. It's the most difficult, critical part of parenting. How do you help create self-confidence in your children when you want to protect them? I learned on the job and from my mistakes.

What I realize, which applies to everyone I may influence, is give as honest and unbiased opinions as I can then get out of the way. I can be there if they stumble or fall. Admit mistakes when you realize them. I trust God to guide my life, so I need to extend that trust to my daughters and anyone else. Following these guidelines is how we help lift others, which honors God's plan for each of us.

Let no one determine your destiny. Be the captain of your life's journey because only you with God's guidance understand where you can and should go. Even when I was wrong, it led me to a better place than if I listened to others and passively followed the standard, accepted road for my disease.

Without this realization, ALS would have ended my life before it started. I would have missed the best and countless blessings God planned for me.

Encourage one another and build each other up.

1 Thessalonians 5:11 (NIV)

9

BE WELL

It is health that is the real wealth, and not pieces of gold and silver.

Mahatma Gandhi

The hardest lesson ALS teaches you in the harshest and most humbling terms imaginable; life is more than the physical aspects of life. This awareness doesn't mean your physical being becomes less vital; it just shifts your perspective on why and how it's essential for living a fulfilling and happy life.

It's hard aging and moving on from the physical perfection of your youthful prime. I was barely past my physical peak when ALS began its relentless assault on my body. Kelsey is now three years from the age I was when my troubles started with ALS. It gives me some perception of how young I was because, as her dad, I cannot fathom her facing such devastation in her life. She's still that cute little girl with a pink outfit with a matching bow in her hair going to her first day of school in my eyes.

ALS reshapes the way you view your physical life when you lose it completely; you comprehend your body is more about how you use it instead of what you accomplish. It doesn't matter what I wore or what personal success and achievement I had.

I grieve losing the freedom to experience the beautiful world where God put us. I regret not doing more with my physical gift to lift others up over my self-aggrandizement.

I mourn not being able to give the physical affection to those my life touches and those I love through a hug, a loving pat, or holding someone's hand. Not sharing simple moments as a husband, father, son, brother, or a friend are what I crave. From going on family trips to working together in a garden to playing games to even cleaning the house and yard are the cherished memories from my childhood. It's the conversations or memorable incidents that came because of these mundane, ordinary tasks that make them special. It's what ALS cruelly stripped away from me. As I delve into taking better care of yourself physically, this is my point-of-view.

Every person I have known with ALS, expresses they wish they had valued and taken better care of their physical health. It has less to do with keeping yourself in peak physical condition than you might think since many people I've known with ALS were competitive athletes when ALS struck. It's more about balance and enjoying your life.

Like many people in their post-high school years, I put on a few pounds since work, and everyday living stresses became a priority. Fast food meals became my norm. The allure of tricking myself that diet soda was a healthy choice became an easy option during my busy days. However, they were lessening my quality of life, a term that becomes significant once ALS enters it. The empty calories weren't sustaining me, so I craved more, leading to weight gain that reduced my ability to enjoy life to the fullest.

It's an easy trap to get caught in, and it becomes a downward spiral that zaps your energy taking away the precious gift you have. Whatever thing you do that is unhealthy and causes the unnecessary decline of your body becomes a source of regret and remorse.

In my first years struggling with ALS, I beat myself up for the moments I wasted not taking better care of my physical body. If I could go back to tell my younger self pay better attention to your body and, more importantly, how I used my healthy body, I would love doing that.

It's simple viewing the mistakes I made in hindsight given the stark reality of the physical challenges I face with ALS. My hope in sharing my story is someone can learn from it; alter their thinking; appreciate and improve their physical health by changing.

Seeing mistakes in reflection when you can't do anything about them causes the saddest regret you experience.

I'm not giving direct advice on how to improve your physical health in this book since that varies for each person. There are libraries of books on health and wellness. One caveat, thoroughly research any health advice because your body is irreplaceable. While ALS made me thoroughly aware of inadequacies in our health and nutrition systems, it's not addressed here. I am giving some essential, common sense guides to help your decisions.

Do it for the right reasons. This remains the most misunderstood concept today. Doing something for your body with only short-range and cosmetic goals leads to failure and disappointment, often creating more damage in the long run. It's appropriate having small targets within a long-term planned change. Even if a short-term event like a wedding causes the transformation, make it a terrific starting point, not the endpoint of your health revolution.

Do it the right way. In today's quick satisfaction, easy solution world, we easily forget this. With all the information at our fingertips, you can become lost and gravitate to the easiest solution. We do not find valuable results in a quick and easy, so if that's the promise made beware. Your body is a precious gift, so shortcut isn't a word we should associate with improving or maintaining it.

Do it for you. Don't undertake to change your body based on someone else's opinion or the false hopes bombarding us daily. That doesn't create happiness. Embark on the journey of improving your physical body for one simple reason, to enhance the life you're living. Any other purpose leads to disappointment since there's always some form of perfection which forever changes, so you never achieve it.

Each new year, people resolve to improve their appearance. You should appreciate and love yourself how you are. God does. If you want to make improvements to yourself, do it to be healthier and live better not to pursue some unrealistic, unachievable picture of perfection portrayed to us each day.

You are beautiful the way you are because of what you possess in your spirit and projecting love with your soul.

Hatred, demeaning and demoralizing yourself or others, no matter how correct you might believe you are, is counter to God's love and beauty. What we need to resolve not as a year goal but as our life goal: find beauty in ourselves, love ourselves then love and find beauty in lives we touch.

Remember, the greatest temple God created is you. The perceived flaws by you or someone else are just perceptions, not His reality. I lost most physical aspects of my life because of ALS, but I recognize this is the way and the truth.

I have chosen to be happy because it is good for my health.

Voltaire

10

AND HAPPY

Begin at once to live and count each separate day as a separate life.

Seneca

When ALS takes hold of your life, it forces you to slow down whether or not that's your desire. As the physical limitations grow greater, your world shrinks. When breathing issues begin, time becomes a precious and fleeting commodity. All this together compels you to live in the moment and value the surrounding people.

Once you're on the precipice of death and remain there as I am on a ventilator, your perspective shifts drastically. No longer do you assume tomorrow comes. You waste little energy on trivial things. When you squander time, you immediately regret misusing the special gift of life God gave you. I would instead seek happiness in whatever form I could rather than waste time wallowing in self-pity and creating misery for myself and others.

It doesn't matter what gloomy circumstances you find yourself in, find joy in life. Be present for the time you're in and use it for your God-given purpose. Revel in the life you enjoy instead of lamenting what you don't control or possess because it's easy falling in the trap of craving what someone else outwardly has. Our society bombards us with the message we cannot be happy if we don't own certain things or live a certain way. The funny fact about that idea, research shows the most satisfied people in the world accept the least and the people with the most, sometimes, they seem the most miserable.

The most blissful experience I had in my pre-ALS life was backpacking in the Rockies with a tent, sleeping bag, and enough food to sustain me. It was roughing it in God's glorious wonder. For me, heaven on earth. My daughter, Kelsey, discovered on a mission trip that the people of Mozambique keep terrific joyful spirits while living on the necessities: food, water, and shelter. I find, counter to the media portrayal, true happiness comes from the interactions we have with each other, not whatever we possess. Even in my state of physical dysfunction, I seem happier than many people whose emphasis is on the wrong things in their lives.

What I miss most because of my physical disability is the ability to start interaction and communication with other people. Not only does it limit my ability to receive happiness, but it also limits my ability to give and help others in a physical sense. I learned to compensate by trying to give what I can mentally, emotionally, and spiritually. What I lacked physically I grew in these areas. Sort of how a blind person has their other senses heightened to offset for their lack of sight. It gives me a way to balance my life and my contribution to others for my lack of physical presence.

Had I given in to the grim reality of my disease, I would miss out on the fantastic prospect of growing into the person God planned on me becoming. That would be tragic.

God wants us to be happy regardless of the situation we find ourselves in. In my worst moments with ALS, when I was enduring not living, He created points of happiness helping me get through. If the negative aspects of my life absorbed me, I would overlook the relief God gave me.

I recognize people struggle with mental health issues that impact their capability to know happiness in their life. I encourage them and everyone to help provide them with the support needed.

When there is a choice, be happy, and help others find happiness because that will bring you blessings of joy beyond imagination. Dedication to the principle of real happiness should be part of the bedrock we build our lives on along with love.

A sad soul can be just as lethal as a germ.

John Steinbeck

11

MOST OF ALL LIVE IN LOVE

Do all the good you can, by all the means you can, in all the ways you can, in all the places you can, at all the times you can, to all the people you can, as long as you can.

John Wesley

A main quest for humans remains why we are here. One episode of the television comedy, Everybody Loves Raymond, examines the meaning of life. When the daughter asks why we're here, it throws their family into a tizzy. The grandparents and uncle become involved leading to a hilarious scene. With the grandmother randomly pulling quotes from the Bible and the adults debating the answer, the uncle in a final moment of frustration looks up and asks why God? His madness is a punchline. However, it represents the doubt we all have.

The episode ends with the parents ready to give a serious response, but the daughter already forgot her question because she's busy laughing and playing with her brothers. It perfectly illustrates how adults confuse the issue while children enjoy life.

What I discovered through my journey with ALS is the answer to the meaning of life is simple. It's for us to love each other. If you need a Biblical guide, Jesus tells us the greatest commandment is to love your neighbor as yourself. No exceptions. Jesus further explains that how you treat the least amongst us is how you treat him. The meaning of life encompasses our purpose in one word, love.

Love Yourself

Love must start with yourself because if you don't love who you are, it limits how fully you give love. It doesn't mean love yourself ignoring the needs of others. Nor is it holding yourself superior to others since it's better to be humble than tooting your own horn. A soaring eagle is far more majestic than a squawking crow. Besides, God recognizes your greatness.

What I mean is don't hold yourself to impossible standards you can never meet. Learn from your mistakes instead of crucifying yourself. Forgive yourself when you take a wrong turn and endeavor to find your right path. It might be difficult. You may even have to create a road to get there, but you become a better person doing it. To love yourself as you are, flaws and all, means you accept you are God's creation because He doesn't make mistakes.

Events in my life caused me to examine it. Why have I struggled? Why have I been unhappy? I realized I got into a rut focusing on things I don't possess like financial security for my family and what ALS has denied me. The self-pity pulled me away from growing into the person God wants me to become, what He desires my life to represent.

For me to become what I'm supposed to evolve into, I must reject anger, bitterness, conflict, and negativity even when pessimism surrounds me. My epiphany occurred when I was struggling and unhappy. The negative emotions choked my spirit.

Some know me as an ALS warrior. I didn't hesitate in the past to take up a sword in the form of my words and go to battle when I felt someone wronged the ALS community. Even when I believed the clash was righteous, the fight would take away my energy. There's a superior path to take, love.

Others may demean, disrespect, and even disregard your life as meaningless. God doesn't. He knows who you are and the wonderment of His creation. Who are they to judge His work? Only jealous fools judge artists like Mozart or Da Vinci. These artists pale compared to your creator. When you love yourself, it opens the possibilities that God created your life's purpose. Loving yourself allows you to better love the people your life touches.

Love Your Neighbors

Love your neighbor seems such a limiting expression to some. They literally view it as meaning their neighborhood or the area they live in. Even within this definition, they have trouble achieving a straightforward principle. How can God expect them to love the neighbor who lets their dog poop in their yard much less the vile, addicted person who makes them uncomfortable? They are shiftless, steal, cause damage, kill, go against everything you value. They bring down your mood, attack your senses, and can even assault you or your family. How can you love someone you want, even desire to hate?

When neighbor means anyone your life indirectly touches; it becomes more complicated. It's impossible when it includes your enemies. You must hate them. Right?

That's the exact purpose of life. Learn to love everyone. Show them love despite whatever perceived flaws they possess because we all have flaws. Some are just better hidden. Give them love to lift them up from whatever is pushing them down, diminishing their light. Create a world around you where anything stays possible for everyone. Make it where the darkness within anyone's soul is impossible to keep from the light hugging them each day. When we commit to doing this, we create a better world, not just for everyone around us, but also for ourselves.

Our lives become less stressful, more productive, and a much happier place to live. There are still storms to weather and obstacles to overcome. However, if each of us strives to live in love, the storms and obstacles won't be of our own making. There won't be the necessity for anyone to take something from you physically, emotionally, mentally, or spiritually. We all will give and receive love.

What if no one else changes? Remember, God wants this from us. Jesus said it's the greatest commandment. Why do we love? Because it's why He created us. Love is the core of our soul. We control the transformation God desires.

I noticed as ALS took over my life, being lonely in my troubles caused me to fall further into despair to hide in my darkness. Loneliness is the root of most problems we confront. It casts a shadow of fear and doubts over our happiness, which over time withers and dies from the lack of light.

Anxiety causes us to lash out and grasp onto anything that fills the cavern loneliness creates in our soul. It does not matter what we grasp onto whether it hurts us or others because the desperate desire to end this loneliness overwhelms everything we do.

There is only one cure for this affliction. Love. Not just receiving love but giving love freely to everyone your life touches. Love is the connection which binds every living thing together in harmony. Love shines a light so bright that nothing can darken our happiness when it's present.

Love doesn't envy, judge, criticize, or harm another. Love accepts all the flaws someone has. You can't give it with strings, rules or even expect to receive love. The only terms associated with love are endless, boundless, infinite, and forgiveness. It's the alpha and omega of life.

Love is the basis of the Christian faith because as Jesus commanded above everything else, we are to love one another. Jesus taught us to love each other, to love our enemies, to love ourselves because that is what He came into this world to teach us. He showed us through His ultimate sacrifice what He expects from us.

I don't know how many days remain for me, but I am dropping all things counter to living in love. I'm taking up the mantle of love following the path Jesus made for me to follow. In today's world, with all the conflict, judgment, bitterness, and negativity, it seems impossible for someone to achieve.

I can tell you based on my life which ALS stripped bare, most things we have convinced people are important aren't. From material things to unrealistic body views to even most of the firmly held beliefs, each of us hold dear are meaningless. Everyone who has their life stripped down as I have; they only desire a few things. Nothing else compares to our connections, mutual understanding, and LOVE both given and received from family, friends, and even strangers.

Love God

Meaning of Life Equation
Loving God = Loving Yourself + Loving Your Neighbors

Even if you don't believe in God, Jesus, any religious belief or higher power, embrace the basic principles of loving yourself and your neighbors. It creates a bountiful world for you and anyone you love. If you're a Christian, love should be your essential guide. We should extend love to everything God created.

By embracing love, you generate a vortex of happiness around you. When happy people surround you, it's tough for sadness to enter your life. If difficult times find you, a life of love builds a shelter against the storms you face. When you confront obstacles, even ones that seem unbearable to overcome, living in love brings you the support you need to conquer anything. You love God because He loves you, He's always with you in this life and the next.

Do not worry about anything, but in everything by prayer and supplication with thanksgiving let your requests be made known to God.

Philippians 4:6 (NRSV)

The principle from Philippians is easier said than done. Countless times I succumbed to the worries of today thinking I alone can solve the problems. The burden was too heavy, my resolve too weak. Each time I faltered and fell under the weight, I asked for God's help. He always assisted. How foolish I must seem to Him waiting until I fell to ask for help. Sometimes I wallowed in my failures too stubborn and embarrassed to ask for aid getting up, but each time God patiently waited until I relented and requested support. He picked me up, dusted me off, and sent me on my way with a loving pat.

ALS entered my life made everything seem unbearable. I couldn't do anything to carry those burdens alone. It was then I slowly understood over 25 years with Lou Gehrig's Disease; God never wanted me to bear anything alone. God is ready and willing to help me, so I NEVER falter much less fall.

That's how much God loves us; He foresees our needs before we ponder them. We need to ask and give thanks. All God asks in return is for us to love Him by loving each other! What a small price for unending, unlimited supporting love.

Forgiveness is the foundation of love since Christ died to forgive our sins, so how can we not excuse the transgressions against us when most are petty and insignificant? That is the purpose of unconditional love. I admit for horrific crimes like murder, violence, or harming a child; I struggle with the concept of forgiveness. People who experienced these unimaginable scenarios found through confronting the perpetrator and finding a way to forgive, it releases their hearts. Through loving mercy, they freed themselves of bitterness, resentment, and hatred that controlled their lives. It brings them peace and love again in the face of the tragedy inflicted on their lives. Love triumphs.

What I believe is if we move toward love, the answer to that struggle becomes easier to understand. The darkness that allows such horrors will shrink, wither, and eventually die or become easier to recognize and contain.

Trust in His love by following the advice of my favorite Sunday school song. It says, "This little light of mine, I'm going to let it shine." I didn't understand this simple song's power until my life's light came close to extinction remaining there for twenty-five years and counting. I discovered the strength and importance of my tiny flickering light. Now, I try letting it become a beacon for anyone who sees it.

ALS provided the fuel that re-ignited my flame. It turned my body into an emaciated shell of what it once was like the older man I saw beginning my story. However, it could not take my spirit. Instead, Lou Gehrig's Disease allowed me to grow mightier in spirit than I would without it.

Don't wait for your ALS to come calling to figure out your reason for living. Shine your light of love on every one your life touches, producing a world for you and others that's free of darkness. God loves you.

Dedicate your life to love, and nothing will be impossible.

Be well and happy, but most of all live in love!

Now choose life
—so that you and your descendants will live—

Deuteronomy 30:19

Dear friends, let's love each other, because love is from God, and everyone who loves is born from God and knows God.

The person who doesn't love does not know God, because God is love.

This is how the love of God is revealed to us: God has sent his only Son into the world so that we can live through him.

This is love: it is not that we loved God but that he loved us and sent his Son as the sacrifice that deals with our sins.

Dear friends, if God loved us this way, we also ought to love each other.

No one has ever seen God.

If we love each other, God remains in us and his love is made perfect in us.

1 John 4:7-12

EPILOGUE

The challenges that stood in my way are substantial since ALS and the disabilities it causes. Overcoming obstacles is an overall theme of the book, so it isn't a shock I had to overcome some significant hurdles writing my story. I didn't expect a major one occurring as I made my final push to finish writing it.

When my computer fried in the fall of 2018, it was discouraging. The circumstances of losing a critical piece of equipment would discourage anyone as they completed a major project. In my case, it took what little independence I have. It also took away my ability to communicate with the outside world. Essentially, it made me face and feel my disability fresh again reopening a painful wound.

Few people understand, even some with my condition, I rarely feel disabled. Since I went on the ventilator and the relentless progression of ALS halted twenty years ago, my life normalized. Except for a few moments each day, I don't think about my disability. It's a true blessing from God.

Being forced to buy a replacement computer near Christmas is not an expense I enjoy taking on, but it's a necessity. I don't fully grasp why God put me through this trial, but I never do. It's something everyone struggles with, why does He allow bad things to happen? We already deal with enough, so why does God let the burden to get heavier?

I no longer dwell on these questions and let them consume me. I learned through the endurance of greater tests in my life to put my trust in God because He never fails, leading me to greener pastures and still waters. Yes, the computer failure frustrated me. As my life returned to normal resuming the final push to complete Living as a Dead Man, I knew there was a reason for it and the time for the book was coming soon.

I'm off to new writing adventures. There is a work of fiction loosely based on generations of my family in Portageville, Missouri. It will center on the life and mystery of a young sharecropper's daughter starting in the early twentieth century until her death at one-hundred and one in 2020.

The follow-up to Living as a Dead Man, titled Philosophy of a Dead Man, builds Section 3 of this book.

ABOUT ALS

The following description is from the
ALS Therapy Development Institute.

https://www.als.net/

Every 90 minutes someone is diagnosed with amyotrophic lateral sclerosis (ALS), a progressive neurodegenerative disorder. Each case is different. ALS, also known as Lou Gehrig's disease, Charcot's disease, and motor neuron disease (MND), attacks specific cells in the brain and spinal cord needed to keep our muscles moving. Early signs and symptoms of ALS include:

muscle cramps and muscle twitching
weakness in hands, legs, feet or ankles
difficulty speaking or swallowing

The senses, including hearing, sight, smell, taste, and touch, are not affected by ALS.

There is no single diagnostic test for ALS. However, experts in the disease, usually neurologists specializing in neuromuscular diseases, are very capable of diagnosing ALS. In some cases, they might order additional tests if the diagnosis is not clear. These include:

electromyography and nerve conduction
magnetic resonance imaging (MRI)
genetic tests
muscle biopsy

161

spinal tap

blood and urine tests

Most people with ALS live 3-5 years after their first signs of disease. About 10% of people with ALS survive at least ten years. This variable rate of disease progression makes prognosis difficult to predict and therapies challenging to develop.

Currently, two medications have been approved by the FDA as treatments for ALS; Riluzole and Radicava. While neither was found in clinical trials to be broadly disease modifying (stopping disease) in all people with ALS, many people taking them do experience some impact on their disease progression.

This urgent unmet medical need for effective treatments for this devastating and fatal disease is the basis for the research and drug development effort at the nonprofit biotech organization, ALS Therapy Development Institute.

In people with ALS, the motor neurons deteriorate, leading to muscle weakness and paralysis. Why these cells are particularly vulnerable remains an open question, but scientists are beginning to unravel how these cells are destroyed, leading to new ways to attack the disease.

When neurologist Jean-Martin Charcot, MD, first peered into the tissues of his patients lost to ALS in 1865, he noticed clear signs of progressive neuronal damage that stretched from the brain to the brain stem (upper motor neurons) to the spinal cord (lower motor neurons) and atrophy of neighboring muscles.

Scientists now understand that this neurodegeneration is exceptionally complicated and occurs through several mechanisms.

There is no single diagnostic tool for ALS. A series of clinical procedures are conducted to rule out neurological conditions whose symptoms closely resemble the disease. In the US, the diagnosis can take about 12 to 14 months. Researchers hope to expedite this process by developing tools that indicate whether people have the disease.

In people with ALS, motor neurons degenerate and become unplugged from neighboring muscles resulting in muscle weakness and muscle atrophy.

Most people with ALS live about 3-5 years after experiencing their first signs of the disease. At least 1 in 10 people live more than ten years following their diagnosis. This variable rate of progression makes predicting prognosis difficult. Clinicians instead rely on regular follow-up visits to monitor people with ALS to manage their disease.

Early signs of ALS

Most people with ALS first feel muscle cramps, spasms or twitching (fasciculations) in one of their arms or legs. Other symptoms include weakness in the hands and feet or loss of balance. This form of the disease is called limb-onset ALS.

About 25% of people with ALS first have trouble talking clearly - slurring words. This form of the disease is called bulbar-onset ALS.

Middle stages of ALS

As the disease spreads, many muscles weaken and start to stiffen. Range of motion exercises will likely be recommended to help keep muscles loose and prevent the formation of contractures and muscle pain.

People with ALS might tire more easily. Breathing may be affected. A BiPAP machine or a phrenic pacer might be suggested, mainly to help improve sleep. A feeding tube might be advised to help meet nutritional needs. Medications might also be recommended to control emotions (pseudobulbar affect) or reduce muscle spasms.

People with bulbar-onset often work with a speech therapist to keep talking longer. People with limb-onset ALS may rely on a cane, walker, or wheelchair due to difficulties walking and maintaining balance.

Late stages of ALS

As the disease progresses, muscles become paralyzed. Most people with ALS require a wheelchair to get around and may communicate through assistive devices using an eye-tracking device or a letter board.

People with late-stage ALS are often cared for in hospices or at home. Some people with ALS choose invasive ventilation to help keep them breathing. Most people lose the battle with ALS due to respiratory failure.

Treatment for ALS

There is no cure for ALS. However, scientists are working hard to develop therapies for this disease. There are currently only two treatments approved by the FDA in the United States. They are riluzole (marketed as Rilutek), and edaravone (sold as Radicava).

Much more is known about the use of Rilutek in ALS as it was approved in the 1990s. Its effects are modest, extending life by about two to three months. More recently, Radicava was approved by the FDA in May 2017, and people with ALS can now access the drug. Clinical trials of Radicava showed the most significant potential impact on maintaining function was in those who started getting infusions of the medication early on in their disease. While neither of these treatments has been shown to halt the progression of ALS, some people who take either or both of them may experience a positive impact on their progression. Both riluzole and edaravone are available today.

ALS is a complex, multi-system disease. A growing number of ALS clinics are deploying multidisciplinary teams to care for people with ALS to meet their physical, emotional, and nutritional needs. These teams include physical, respiratory, speech, and occupational therapists to help people with ALS breathe more comfortable, keep moving, and stay connected. Palliative care specialists support people with ALS and their care providers.

Today, there are dozens of clinical trials evaluating potential treatments enrolling people with ALS and their families. For more information on enrollment and inclusion criteria, visit our clinical trials page.

Emerging medicines

Researchers are developing several treatment strategies to fight ALS. Immune system-modulating drugs including Anelixis Therapeutics AT-1501 and Neuraltus Pharmaceuticals' NP001 hope to slow ALS in its tracks by reducing neuroinflammation. Stem cell-based strategies including Cedar Sinai's GDNF trial, Neuralstem's NSI-566, Brainstorm's NurOwn hope to shield motor neurons from destruction. And, potential muscle boosters, including Cytokinetics' tirasemtiv (CK-357) hope to help people breathe easier and keep muscles moving. Edaravone (Radicut/Radicava) was approved for use in Japan against ALS in 2015 is before the FDA for approval in 2017. There are many other potential treatments in the works in earlier stage clinical trials that are also seeking volunteers.

Scientists are also repurposing medicines in hopes of bringing ALS therapies more quickly to the clinic. The FDA-approved heart medicine mexiletine might slow ALS by reducing hyperexcitability, a potentially early step in the disease. The multiple sclerosis medicine, Novartis' Gilenya, aims to treat ALS by reducing neuroinflammation.

There are also a growing number of medicines that might help alleviate key symptoms of the disease. Baclofen may reduce muscle spasms. Nuedexta might help keep emotions in check (pseudobulbar affect). Mexiletine might reduce painful muscle cramps. Several medicines, including Robinul, Elavil, and Botox, may help reduce salivation.

Care and management

Breathing devices may also improve quality of life and extend survival. Non-invasive ventilators such as a BiPAP machine help people with ALS breathe better, sleep better, and boost survival by about a year according to some estimates. Phrenic pacers (NeuRX DPS) might also help people sleep better and extend survival according to clinical observations about 16 months after NIV use is initiated. Clinical trials are ongoing to further evaluate the NeuRX DPS and identify which people with ALS might benefit from them.

Certain forms of exercise are also becoming routine. Range of motion (stretching) is the general practice for people with ALS to prevent muscle pain and the formation of contractures. Emerging aerobic workouts might improve quality of life and help reduce functional decline. A clinical trial evaluating the benefits of certain forms of exercises, including stationary cycling and weight training remains ongoing.

HeadMouse and Dragger/SofType Software

http://www.orin.com/access/headmouse/index.htm

I used a HeadMouse by Origin along with their Dragger and SofType software to write this book. I have used this method to access my computer for over twenty years, including during my years at the University of Michigan-Dearborn as a full-time graduate student.

A HeadMouse replaces the standard computer mouse for people who cannot use or have limited use of their hands. The HeadMouse translates natural movements of a user's head into directly proportional mouse pointer movement – move your head, and the mouse pointer follows along. The HeadMouse has a wireless optical sensor which tracks a tiny disposable target worn by the user on his/her forehead, glasses, or even a hat. It works just like a computer mouse, with the mouse pointer being controlled by head movement.

The HeadMouse will track head movement with the user comfortably located anywhere in front of his/her computer display. With HeadMouse Nano's high tracking resolution, pixel-precise control is available to everyone. This precision allows a user to perform such tasks as drawing, photo editing, graphic illustration, and Computer Aided Design (CAD).

With HeadMouse Nano and an on-screen keyboard, a person with disabilities can use any application – everything begins with access.

Selections and mouse button operations can be performed using a variety of adaptive switches, including Origin Instruments Sip/Puff Switch, Orby,™ and mouse button software, such as Dragger.™ Using Dragger, mouse clicks are performed by positioning the pointer and dwelling for a selectable period of time. HeadMouse

Nano has an integrated infrared receiver for adaptive wireless switches, using our available Beam.™

When used with an on-screen keyboard such as SofType™ or KeyStrokes,™ HeadMouse provides access to the full range of keyboard and mouse functions.

The tiny Target Dot is typically worn on the forehead, glasses frame or the brim of a ball cap.

Dragger™ and AutoClick™

Dragger is a software utility for manipulating the left, right, and middle mouse buttons of a standard mouse or mouse emulator, like the HeadMouse®, often utilized by people who have physical motor challenges. Dragger can be used to enter mouse clicks via direct selection (usually with an adaptive switch) and by holding the mouse pointer motionless which is commonly referred to as "dwell." The dwell selection function in Dragger is called AutoClick™. When enabled, AutoClick monitors the pointer and clicks the left mouse button when the pointer is brought to rest for the programmable dwell time. If the pointer remains motionless, it will not click again. Using the Dragger toolbar this single left click can be turned into a Double Click, Right Click, Middle Click, or Left, Right and Middle Drag.

SofType

SofType is a software utility which replaces the functionality of a desktop keyboard with a full-featured, on-screen keyboard. SofType can be accessed using a mouse or mouse emulator such as the HeadMouse® Nano. SofType works by generating an image of a keyboard on the computer screen. When a key is selected (clicked), the character represented by that key is sent to the Windows application with focus.

ALS Organizations & Websites

The following ALS organizations and websites (social media groups) have filled in gaps by providing equipment and services not covered or offered essential connections to others dealing with ALS. These connections formed what I lovingly call my ALS family. The list provided is not every organization and websites; just the ones I can remember and are active today. Any omission of organizations is only due to my twenty-five year plus journey and the memory lapses caused by time.

ALS Organizations

Team Gleason – http://www.teamgleason.org/

ALS-TDI – https://www.als.net/

ALS Association – http://www.alsa.org/

ALSA Mid-America Chapter – https://www.alsa-midamerica.org/

ALSA St. Louis Chapter – http://www.alsa-stl.org/

MDA – https://www.mda.org/

Patients Like Me – https://www.patientslikeme.com/

ALS Ride for Life – https://alsrideforlife.org/

National ALS Registry – https://www.cdc.gov/als/

ALS News Today – https://alsnewstoday.com/

Augie's Quest – https://augiesquest.org/

Susan Mast ALS Foundation – https://www.susanmastals.org/

I AM ALS – https://iamals.org/

Facebook Groups

https://www.facebook.com/groups/livingwithalsPALS/

https://www.facebook.com/groups/ALSnews/

https://www.facebook.com/groups/livingwithals/